XML, HTML, XHTML MAGIC

By Molly E. Holzschlag

Contributors: Martin L. de Vore, Steve Franklin, John Kuhlman, Christopher Schmitt, Jason Cranford Teague

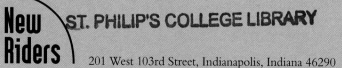

New Riders

ST. PHILIP'S COLLEGE LIBRARY

201 West 103rd Street, Indianapolis, Indiana 46290

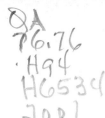

XML, HTML, XHTML Magic

Copyright © 2002 by New Riders Publishing

International Standard Book Number: 0-7357-1139-9

Library of Congress Catalog Card Number: 20-01088187

Printed in the United States of America

First Printing: September 2001

06 05 04 03 02   7 6 5 4 3 2 1

Interpretation of the printing code: The rightmost double-digit number is the year of the book's printing; the rightmost single-digit number is the number of the book's printing. For example, the printing code 02-1 shows that the first printing of the book occurred in 2002.

Trademarks

Warning and Disclaimer

Publisher
David Dwyer

Associate Publisher
Al Valvano

Executive Editor
Stephanie Wall

Product Marketing Manager
Kathy Malmloff

Managing Editor
Kristy Knoop

Acquisitions Editor
Linda Anne Bump

Development Editor
Linda Laflamme

Project Editor
Suzanne Pettypiece

Copy Editor
Sheri Replin

Technical Editor
Jon Steffey
Steve Franklin

Cover Designer
Aren Howell

Interior Designer
Steve Gifford

Compositor
Ron Wise

Proofreader
Katherine Shull

Indexer
Lisa Stumpf

CONTENTS AT A GLANCE

ABOUT THE AUTHOR

Molly E. Holzschlag is an author, instructor, and designer who brings warmth and enthusiasm to her books, lectures, and web sites. Widely known for her recent stint at WebReview.com as Executive Editor, and honored as one of the Top 25 Most Influential Women on the web, Molly has spent more than a decade working in the online world. She has written and contributed to 18 books about web design and markup languages. Molly holds a master of arts in media studies from the New School for Social Research. She is also a digital artist, a creative writer, and a musician playing with the original acoustic duo Courage Sisters.

ABOUT THE CONTRIBUTORS

Martin L. de Vore has been involved with computers since 1982 when he taught people how to access and download limericks from the University of New Mexico's UNIX system's "fortunes" file. With the purchase of his first home computer in 1986, a Commodore 128, he participated in Commodore's Quantum Link online service, which later evolved into AOL. In the early 1990s, Martin was busy exploring the Internet, experimenting with the construction of "gopher holes" until he constructed his first web site in February 1995. Since that time, he has been constantly online, helping others construct web sites, engaging in sometimes-spirited discussions with members of the markup language communities, and experimenting with new technologies. A 1986 graduate of the University of New Mexico, Martin is currently employed as the managing editor of the Observer newspaper group in the northeastern Houston, Texas, area. Prior to that, he was employed as a programmer for the Harris County Precinct 4.

John Kuhlman is the executive producer and founder of Kreativworks, www.kreativeworks.com/. Prior to launching the studio in 2000, he worked in a funky dual capacity as the speech writer and publicity hack for the Nevada Board of Regents and as the "web dude" for the University and Community College System of Nevada. John also served a four-year tour of duty as the communications director for United Way, where he managed both online and offline marketing and advertising campaigns as well as direct mail promotions.

Christopher Schmitt is working on a handful of forthcoming online web design and development guides. During the day, he works for MindComet as senior design technologist and production lead on various client projects. Visit his personal site at www.christopher.org.

Jason Cranford Teague is a Senior Information Architect for Lante, and was previously with iXL where he designed web sites for WebMD, Coca-Cola, CNN, BellSouth, DuPont, Kodak, Synovus, and The Technology Association of Georgia. His books include the best-selling *How To Program HTML Frames: Interface Design and JavaScript* and *DHTML and CSS for the World Wide Web*, which is consistently one of the top-selling books on DHTML. Visit Jason's web site at www.webbedenvironments.com.

Steve Franklin has been involved with Internet and related technologies for more than a decade. His technical interests include web architectures, software design, and data storage. He also has a strong interest in search engine technology, which he shares at www.lookoff.com.

ABOUT THE TECH EDITOR

Jon Steffey has taught web development for more than five years through WestLake Internet Training and as an independent consultant. Jon has authored training classes on HTML, CGI Scripting, and Database Integration with Perl, Active Server Pages, Java Servlets, XML, and other technologies. He has participated in the development of both public web sites and custom-built intranet applications. Prior to teaching web development, he taught high school English, and looks forward to teaching in the public schools again. Jon lives in Pittsburgh, PA, with his wife and son and can be reached at jonrsteffey@yahoo.com.

DEDICATION

For my family

ACKNOWLEDGMENTS

First and foremost, I want to thank the great authors who jumped to help with this book. All the real magic here is because of them. So thank you Martin, Steve, John, Christopher, and Jason.

I am grateful to Linda Bump for being an expert shepherdess and guiding the book through its process. Linda Laflamme certainly had her hands full with this project. She helped shape the book with grace and calm. A note of special gratitude for my technical editors, Jon Steffey and Steve Franklin. Their careful and thoughtful insights helped make this book technically more accurate and useful to readers.

As always, to my family, friends, and supporters for making my world go 'round.

A Message from New Riders

As the reader of this book, you are our most important critic and commentator. We value your opinion and want to know what we're doing right, what we could do better, in what areas you'd like to see us publish, and any other words of wisdom you're willing to pass our way.

As Executive Editor at New Riders, I welcome your comments. You can fax, email, or write me directly to let me know what you did or didn't like about this book—as well as what we can do to make our books better. When you write, please be sure to include this book's title, ISBN, and author, as well as your name and phone or fax number. I will carefully review your comments and share them with the authors and editors who worked on the book.

Please note that I cannot help you with technical problems related to the topic of this book, and that due to the high volume of email I receive, I might not be able to reply to every message. Thanks.

Email: stephanie.wall@newriders.com

Mail: Stephanie Wall
         Executive Editor
         New Riders Publishing
         201 West 103rd Street
         Indianapolis, IN 46290 USA

Visit Our Web Site: www.newriders.com

On our web site, you'll find information about our other books, the authors we partner with, book updates and file downloads, promotions, and a calendar of trade shows and other professional events with which we'll be involved. We hope to see you around.

Email Us from Our Web Site

Go to www.newriders.com and click on the Contact link if you

- Have comments or questions about this book.

- Want to report errors that you have found in this book.

- Have a book proposal or are interested in writing for New Riders.

- Would like us to send you one of our author kits.

- Are an expert in a computer topic or technology and are interested in being a reviewer or technical editor.

- Want to find a distributor for our titles in your area.

- Are an educator/instructor who wants to preview New Riders books for classroom use. In the body/comments area, include your name, school, department, address, phone number, office days/hours, text currently in use, and enrollment in your department, along with your request for either desk/examination copies or additional information.

Call Us or Fax Us

You can reach us toll-free at (800) 571-5840 + 9 + 3500 (ask for New Riders). If outside the U.S., please call 1-317-581-3500 and ask for New Riders. If you prefer, you can fax us at 1-317-581-4663, Attention: New Riders.

Technical Support for This Book/Customer Support Issues

Although we encourage entry-level users to get as much as they can out of our books, keep in mind that our books are written assuming a non-beginner level of user-knowledge of the technology. This assumption is reflected in the brevity and shorthand nature of some of the tutorials.

New Riders will continually work to create clearly written, thoroughly tested and reviewed technology books of the highest educational caliber and creative design. We value our customers more than anything—that's why we're in this business—but we cannot guarantee to each of the thousands of you who buy and use our books that we will be able to work individually with you through tutorials or content with which you may have questions. We urge readers who need help in working through exercises or other material in our books—and who need this assistance immediately—to use as many of the resources that our technology and technical communities can provide, especially the many online user groups and list servers available.

INTRODUCTION

Web markup is in a state of profound change. You can write web documents in HTML, XHTML, and even XML with style in some instances. However, each of these options demands knowledge about the markup in question—especially if you are going to create pages that make the most of today's technology while still maintaining backward compatibility. The primary goal of this book is to show people familiar with HTML how and when to work more effectively in HTML, begin moving toward XHTML, and, perhaps most important, learn to incorporate style sheets, working toward a clear separation of document formatting and presentation. This move is essential for many reasons. First, XHTML is now the official recommended web markup language, and for many reasons, using it as much as possible sends a message to other authors, web browser manufacturers, and software developers that we are ready for the most interoperable, standardized methodologies available. After all, this makes our lives easier.

Beyond the issue of recommendations is the reason why learning HTML, XHTML, and style is the easiest, least-painful means of expanding your skills as the web grows and changes. You'll find that XHTML makes learning XML and XML applications easier because it works with a vocabulary in which you are already familiar: HTML.

Working on WebReview.com was the perfect testing ground for me (see Chapter 3, " Managing a Weekly Publication"). In the process of updating the site to be more contemporary, I found that there were certain things with markup that I could not do in valid HTML or XHTML 1.0. In order to aim toward the goal of clean markup documents and achieve an attractive look, I challenged myself to rethink what I knew about web design and development, and face some choices regarding which technologies were most appropriate for the circumstances.

Combining markup, style, scripting, and server technologies is tough stuff. Yet the growing web designer will find that he or she is greatly empowered when an understanding of the rules combined with a good dose of innovative, creative thinking occurs. This book helps you to easily understand contemporary perspectives on web design and also provide exciting, colorful techniques and tips that will inspire you to try new things with your web sites.

Is designing for the web more complex than ever? I believe so. Do we sometimes break rules? Yes, we do. But, we're empowered when we know which rules we're breaking and why. What's more, an understanding of present-day thinking combined with real-world examples can be profoundly helpful in getting you thinking like a strategist while developing like a pro.

WHO WE ARE

When I considered what would give this book a global perspective on current markup and related technologies, it became clear that I'd have to turn to people who are actually working in the field everyday and having to adjust to monumental change and challenge. As a result, I only chose contributors who could make the book a richer experience. We come from different backgrounds: Martin L. de Vore is a content specialist; John Kuhlman serves a range of client needs from print to web; Christopher Schmitt cut his teeth interning for David Siegel and has continued on to create his own niche in seeking the fine balance between visual design and technical functionality; Jason Cranford Teague has a special interest in DHTML and scripting; and Steve Franklin has an interest in WAP and wireless projects. What we all share in common is that we each work daily to create professional web sites. So the information shared in this book comes from hard-won, real-world experience.

WHO YOU ARE

You're either working on the web professionally or you're interested in doing so. Either way, you have a basic familiarity with HTML and probably have used CSS. If you're just getting started with markup, fear not—Chapter 1, " About Web Markup: XML, HTML, XHTML," provides a great jumping-off place for you. No matter what your expertise, you're looking for a new level of understanding to help move you forward in your web site design and developmental goals, and do so with a contemporary, yet sensible, approach. This book serves to inspire you to do just that.

WHAT'S IN THIS BOOK

XML, HTML, XHTML Magic consists of three main parts: Markup, Popular Sites, and Professional Sites.

Part I, "Markup," gives you the foundations you need and want to know. You'll review (or learn, for those readers not yet familiar) how HTML, XML, XHTML are all related. This section is a must-read for all web designers and developers because we show you how to place markup into context, answer some critical questions about XML, and help you clearly understand how to use Cascading Style Sheets (CSS) with markup to make recommendation-compliant, highly interoperable sites.

Whether it's news, a corporate identity, a graphics-intensive site, or a personal site, information has to be properly organized. The lessons in Part II of this book, "Popular Sites," help you to gain a sense of that organization in the context of the types of sites that you're most likely designing.

But markup doesn't exist on its own. In fact, to really create sites that appeal to audiences, you'll want to have a variety of tools from which to choose. In Part III, "Professional Sites," the focus shifts to effective commerce, community, and wireless, relying on an integration of markup and other technologies, such as PHP and WAP. It's a section both rooted in the needs of today, yet reaching for the goals of a rapidly approaching tomorrow.

Throughout this book, you have the opportunity to experience the wisdom of designers and developers who show you techniques and technologies that are part of any web adventurer's contemporary toolbox. You learn about color, type, and layout; using server technologies to make your sites interactive, employing tools like Blogger to keep sites fresh and interesting. You even learn a bit about e-commerce and XML applications, such as the Wireless Markup Language (WML) for wireless site development. All the info you need to make some magic of your own—and then some!

> **Tip:** You'll want to drop by this book's web site at www.xhtml-resources.com /magic/. On the site, you'll find the full code and components you'll need for the projects in this book, as well as information about this book, its authors, updates, corrections, resources, and a feedback area to let us know what you think.

OUR ASSUMPTIONS AS WE WROTE THIS BOOK

As mentioned, we believe readers of this book:

- Have a familiarity with HTML
- Have probably used CSS
- Are adept at testing pages in a variety of web browsers
- Understand how to create web graphics
- Are interested in web markup
- Are interested in creating pages that conform to current World Wide Web Consortium (W3C) Recommendations
- Have some awareness of platform types (Windows, Mac, and Unix/Linux)

Although we recommend some tools along the way (and you'll have to inquire with your ISP to see if certain server-side services are available) as long as you have a text editor such as Notepad or SimpleText, an imaging program (preferably Photoshop), and a web browser, you can begin working on projects immediately.

CONVENTIONS USED IN THIS BOOK

Every computer book has its own style of presenting information. As you flip through this book, you'll notice that we have an interesting layout. Because we know most of you are really into visual learning, the emphasis is on the code and its visual results. The real meat of the projects starts in the next section. Take a look:

In the left column, you'll find step-by-step instructions for completing the project and succinct, but extremely valuable, explanations. The text next to the number contains the action that you must perform. In many cases, the action text is followed by a paragraph that contains contextual information. Note that if you want to perform the steps quickly and without any background info, read only the text next to the step numbers.

In the corresponding columns to the right, you'll find code and screen shots illustrating the steps. You'll also find Notes and Tips, which provide you with additional contextual information or customization techniques.

To help you more easily find the code you need to type in to make the book's projects work, we've color-coded it for you. Code that makes up the framework is in orange. Code that you enter to customize your site is printed in black

At the end of each project, you'll find unique customization information. Each Magic project is designed to be highly customizable. We provide as many tips and examples of what you can do with the techniques you've learned, so that you can apply them to your own work quickly and easily.

XML, XHTML, HTML Magic showcases how working web designers and developers solve problems and address concerns regarding how web sites are built. The angle is real world, but progressive in that it teaches you sophisticated approaches to markup, style sheets, and integration of other technologies, such as PHP, WAP, and WML.

PART I

MARKUP

ABOUT WEB MARKUP:
XML, HTML, XHTML

"Apathy can be overcome by enthusiasm, and

enthusiasm can only be aroused by two things:

first, an ideal, which takes the imagination by

storm, and second, a definite intelligible plan

for carrying that ideal into practice."

—ARNOLD TOYNBEE

There's no doubt that you're anxious to jump in and begin using XML, HTML, or XHTML to add magic to your web pages. But before you dive into the actual projects, you need to understand a little bit about the concepts and goals of successful markup.

Even for those who use markup every day, the likelihood is that the historical and conceptual aspect of markup is not something that you studied. After all, most web authors bootstrapped their way into the industry and learned how to mark up documents by using available resources. A more formal education simply hasn't been possible in our rush to build the web.

But why is paying attention to markup technology even important? After all, you probably created pages and sites that work just fine. Well, there are several important reasons why understanding markup and recommended approaches to creating web pages makes sense. Here are a few of the strongest reasons:

- **Following W3C (*World Wide Web Consortium*)-recommended markup approaches creates consistency between documents**—This, in turn, saves you time and frustration when you're trying to find errors within a document. What's more, if you have multiple people working on a site, adhering to standard practices creates a more efficient work environment.

- **If you're frustrated by browser and platform inconsistencies, you'll find that following recommendations (along with some common sense) will eliminate many of your struggles**—Documents become more interoperable, which reduces testing time and increases the portability of documents.

- **Documents that conform to W3C recommendations pay attention to the needs of the disabled**—This ensures that the information within those documents can be accessed easily and understood clearly.

- **The web is "world" wide—something we occasionally forget!**—Formal markup provides a means by which documents can be prepared to display in a variety of languages using different character sets.

- **As people move from web to wireless and alternative means of accessing web-based data, clean markup becomes imperative**—Markup that adheres to current recommendations and approaches can easily be interpreted by a much wider range of user agents beyond the browser, which makes your information widely accessible.

This chapter helps get all readers on the same page (if you'll pardon the terrible pun) in terms of markup and style, and helps provide a stable platform upon which to develop fantastic sites.

WHAT IS HTML?

To understand HTML, you need to step back to its parent markup language, the *Standard Generalized Markup Language* (SGML). SGML has been around for years, and it's become a standard for document-markup specialists in government and, especially, industries such as medicine, law, and finance.

SGML is referred to as a "meta" language. It exists to create other markup languages. SGML is essentially a collection of language rules that authors use to create their own document languages. HTML is one of the resulting languages—a child, if you will, of its meta-parent SGML.

HTML took SGML's structure, syntax, and basic rules. However, HTML, even in its current seemingly complex state, is much less complex and detailed than SGML. In its early life, HTML was very simple. It existed to allow for some basic markup of pages for the web, including paragraphs, line breaks, and headers. (Remember, the web was first a text-only environment.) HTML was not developed with presentation concerns in mind. Rather, its goal was to present information. Enter the visual browser, which changed the web environment from a place of constructed text documents to a place that promised opportunities for visual design. HTML, and web browsers themselves, were stretched out of proportion in order to accommodate the rapid-fire pace of the web's visual and interactive growth. Designers, obviously, were naturally more concerned with creating designs that were visually rich and esthetically pleasing.

Trying to manipulate HTML to get it to do what you want can be frustrating. No consistent methods exist for creating a layout. For example, to lay out a page in columns, you rely on tables, instead of style-sheet positioning because, in most instances, you must create cross-browser compatibility for the designs. You also have little control over white space—relying on workarounds, such as single-pixel spacer GIFs—and there's essentially no stable way to manage type. HTML is, in many ways, a designer's nightmare because the web was never meant to be a graphical environment. But it became one, and how to manage that reality has been a challenge ever since.

THE INFLUENCE OF XML

Another child of SGML is *Extensible Markup Language* (XML). Interestingly, XML is also a meta language. It exists as a means of creating other languages. While SGML is a complex meta language and is extremely detailed, XML has emerged as a streamlined meta language that's suitable for creating web-markup applications that are customizable and flexible for the needs of specific applications. Examples of XML markup applications include *Scalable Vector Graphics* (SVG), *Synchronized Multimedia Integration Language* (SMIL), and *Wireless Markup Language* (WML).

People who work on the evolution of markup languages through the *World Wide Web Consortium* (W3C) began to look at HTML and the problems it faced due to the stretching and manipulating to accommodate design. Donning the glasses of XML, it becomes clear to see that HTML was, in many ways, a linguistic markup mess. So, the W3C worked to take the best of HTML and apply the strength and logic of XML. From this effort came a new, refined markup language, the *Extensible Hypertext Markup Language* (XHTML).

XHTML is the reformulation of HTML as an XML application. In other words, the rules and methodologies of XML are applied to HTML. This brings syntactical strength back into HTML, which lost that strength during its rapid evolution from text-document markup language to the de facto language of visual design. By strengthening markup in this way, markup is closer to the interoperable, accessible, international, and growth-oriented goals mentioned at the beginning of this chapter.

TRANSITIONING FROM HTML TO XHTML

Because XHTML is the current recommended markup language of the W3C, many authors are beginning to transitioning their practices to XHTML. As you work through this book, you'll see many examples of this. However, XHTML is not always the best choice because it is often stricter than HTML 4. So, it takes experience and understanding to be able to choose which markup methodology you're going to use.

To balance shifting trends, and approach the demand for better standardization across browsers, HTML 4 emerged with some potent rules. Your challenge as a developer: These rules, in their strictest incarnation, don't always work in cross-browser/cross-platform design, and they are often not backward compatible.

BASIC MARKUP SYNTAX: ELEMENTS, ATTRIBUTES, AND VALUES

The central pillar of all web markup commands is the element. Markup elements are made up of a tag or a tag combination plus any content. A tag is the identity of an element; it says, "Do this." But tags become powerful with modification, and that modification begins with an attribute.

Attributes are similar to verbs; they promote action. With them, the tag can suddenly come to life and not only do something, but do it in a certain way. An attribute is made up of an *attribute name* and an *attribute value*. Attributes must be modified by *values*. A value defines the way an attribute will act.

Think of an adverb that modifies an action: How did John run? John ran quickly! Values add concepts, such as "quickly," which tells the tag and the attribute, not only what and how, but to what specific degree.

Metaphorically, the sentence, "John ran quickly" equals the basic syntactical structure of markup. "John" is equivalent of a tag, "ran" is like an attribute name, and "quickly" is the attribute value ascribed to that attribute, which ultimately describes the way in which the tag behaves.

To address these issues, HTML 4 has built-in accommodations for them. Interestingly, it is this flexibility within HTML 4 that is the least understood—and yet it's a seminal aspect of the HTML 4 recommendation.

These accommodations are referred to as "interpretations" of HTML 4, and they fall into one of the following three document type definitions (DTD):

- **Strict HTML 4**—This is the most pure of HTML 4 interpretations. Anything deprecated (condemned) or made obsolete in this version of the language is not ever used. The strict interpretation is also the most optimistic version of HTML 4 because many of its rules are far ahead of the stability user agents, or browsers, offer.

- **Transitional, or "loose," HTML 4**—By combining aspects of the prior version of HTML (HTML 3.2) with elements from the strict HTML 4 standard, a more realistic, useable version of the language emerges. Here you find the most backward compatibility for many public and contemporary web site designs.

- **Frameset HTML 4**—This includes all the information within the transitional version combined with frame-based elements, such as FRAMESET. The frameset interpretation exists as an interpretation to confirm the standardization of frames within HTML and offer a regulated method of using them.

The standard expects that you will insert the appropriate document version and the *document type definition* (DTD) (see the section, "Features of XHTML") information that identifies the standard to which the document conforms. So, if you're creating a strict HTML document, the shell of the document will appear with the document version, as shown in Listing 1.1.

Transitional documents will appear with the document type and structure demonstrated in Listing 1.2.

Finally, any page you build with frames in HTML 4 must be denoted as being within the frameset interpretation. Frameset documents will contain the frameset version information, as follows:

```
<!DOCTYPE HTML PUBLIC "-//W3C//DTD HTML 4.0 Frameset//EN"
"http://www.w3.org/TR/REC-html40/frameset.dtd">
```

Along with these interpretations, the W3C encourages authors to adopt three primary concepts. These concepts exist to ameliorate problems and concerns with the language's past (and often current) use:

- **Separate document structure from presentation and style**—Much of HTML 4 focuses on taking any element from prior language versions used for presentation or style of information and setting it aside. Instead, style sheets for presentation and design are typically recommended.

- **Think carefully about accessibility and internationalization**—Because HTML was originally built for all people to access documents, including those on a variety of platforms, using different languages, different user agents, and with a special concern for those having physical impairments, the standard asks that you keep these issues in mind when authoring code. A good example of this is adding alt attribute descriptions to img tags, which helps visually impaired users better understand web documents.

- **Make documents load more quickly through careful table design**—HTML 4 has several element additions that help tables render incrementally. In fact, HTML 4 highly encourages developers to move away from using tables for an underlying grid system, implementing the use of style sheet positioning in its place. Of course, choosing to use style positioning over table grid systems is difficult to achieve. Style sheet positioning is highly unstable and unreliable, and there's no backward compatibility built in.

LISTING 1.1   SAMPLE HTML STRICT DOCUMENT

```
<!DOCTYPE HTML PUBLIC "-//W3C//DTD HTML 4.0//EN"
"http://www.w3.org/TR/REC-html40/strict.dtd">
<html>
<head>
<title>Strict HTML Sample Shell</title>
</head>
<body>

</body>
</html>
```

LISTING 1.2   SAMPLE HTML TRANSITIONAL DOCUMENT

```
<!DOCTYPE HTML PUBLIC "-//W3C//DTD HTML 4.0 Transitional//EN"
"http://www.w3.org/TR/REC-html40/loose.dtd">
<html>
<head>
<title>Strict HTML Sample Shell</title>
</head>
<body>

</body>
</html>
```

Now, XHTML 1.0 builds heavily on these foundations. Whether you choose to employ XHTML or HTML, the bottom line is that you should use recommended markup rather than arbitrary markup. This is especially important when you move from HTML into the realm of XML and beyond, because without the foundational concepts and techniques, you run the risk of making mistakes, such as introducing proprietary or even non-existing markup into a document. If that happens, and you try to share it with another colleague or company, significant, time-consuming problems can ensue.

FEATURES OF **XHTML**

As you delve deeper into XHTML, you begin to see how it uses aspects of both familiar HTML concepts, and strict ideas influenced by XML. In XHTML, document conformance and DTDs are essentials; this is also true of valid HTML.

Document Conformance and DTDs

In order for a document to conform to XHTML 1.0, it must adhere to the following:

- The document must validate against one of the three DTDs: strict, transitional, or frameset.
- The root element of an XHTML 1.0 document is `<html>`.
- The root element designates an XHTML namespace by using the `xmlns` attribute.
- A DOCTYPE (DTD) must appear in the document prior to the root element.

A recommended, but not absolutely necessary, component to XHTML 1.0 documents is the XML declaration `<?xml>`. The XML declaration defines the document as an XML document and describes the XML version. Some XHTML authors leave the XML declaration out because many browsers do not understand it, and it will cause the code to render improperly or not render at all if used.

A problem exists with leaving the XML declaration out, however. Because the XML declaration allows you to specify the character encoding within a document (this is important for documents that use non-ASCII encoding), leaving it out

means your pages are vulnerable to improper rendering of special characters. As a workaround, you can include a `meta` tag in the head portion of your document that defines the character encoding you're using (this will usually be UTF-8 or UTF-16):

```
<meta http-equiv="Content-Type" content="text/html;charset=UTF-8" />
```

> **Warning:** This `meta` workaround for character encoding only works for UTF-8 or UTF-16 (standard ASCII characters). If you are using any other encoding method, you must include the XML declaration for the encoding to work.

You will see examples in this book that include the XML declaration, that do not include the declaration, and that do or do not use the `meta` tag workaround. It's important that you determine which approach is best for your unique needs. If you're working on documents in English, you won't need to worry too much. However, if you are creating documents by using other character sets, such as those in Japanese for example, you'll need to research and employ the appropriate character set. You can do this with a visit to http://www.unicode.org/.

As mentioned earlier, the vocabulary rule sets used in web markup are called DTDs. In XHTML 1.0, as with HTML 4, only three preset DTDs exist. How you write your XHTML documents and how they're validated by various tools relies on the DTD you choose.

In XML, and for future versions of XHTML, DTDs can be customized. This adds a great deal of power to your toolkit because you can define the rules and the actual tags that a document must use to conform to that common language. So, if a company makes a special product, they can create their own vocabulary to manage that product. Or entire industries, such as medical or financial, can share DTDs specific to their unique needs.

The three DTDs currently available for your use in XHTML 1.0 are

- Strict
- Transitional
- Frameset

You should immediately recognize these DTDs; they are the same as in HTML 4.01. The actual vocabularies are somewhat different, however, which reflects the rigor and syntactical shifts that occurred in XHTML since HTML became an XML application.

Strict XHTML 1.0 is the most rigorous, and the most pure of XHTML 1.0 syntax. When writing a strict XHTML 1.0 document, you'll use the strict DOCTYPE declaration, as follows:

```
<!DOCTYPE html PUBLIC "-//W3C//DTD XHTML 1.0 Strict//EN" "DTD/xhtml1-strict.dtd">
```

Listing 1.3 shows a strict and conforming XHTML 1.0 document.

Transitional XHTML 1.0 is the more forgiving vocabulary. This forgiveness appears in general concepts rather than syntactical adherence. In other words, you must follow syntax rules and rules for well-formed documents. But, you do have leeway with certain elements, attributes, and code approaches. For example, in transitional XHTML 1.0, you can use deprecated tags, such as font or center. These tags are considered presentational and are, therefore, unavailable in the strict DTD.

Transitional XHTML 1.0 documents use the transitional DOCTYPE declaration:

```
<!DOCTYPE html PUBLIC "-//W3C//DTD XHTML 1.0 Transitional//EN"
"DTD/xhtml1-transitional.dtd">
```

Listing 1.4 provides a look at a transitional XHTML 1.0 document.

The frameset DTD denotes a document as a frameset. Any frameset you create in XHTML 1.0 must be declared as such or it will not validate. The frameset DTD in XHTML 1.0 requires the following DOCTYPE declaration:

```
<!DOCTYPE html PUBLIC "-//W3C//DTD XHTML 1.0 Frameset//EN" "DTD/xhtml1-frameset.dtd">
```

Listing 1.5 is a frameset document in XHTML 1.0.

LISTING 1.4   A TRANSITIONAL XHTML 1.0 SHELL

```
<?xml version="1.0"?>
<!DOCTYPE html PUBLIC "-//W3C//DTD XHTML 1.0 Transitional//EN"
"DTD/xhtml1-transitional.dtd">
<html xmlns="http://www.w3.org/1999/xhtml">
<head>
<title>Transitional Document Sample</title>

</head>
<body>


</body>
</html>
```

LISTING 1.3   A STRICT AND CONFORMING XHTML 1.0 SHELL

```
<?xml version="1.0"?>
<!DOCTYPE html PUBLIC "-//W3C//DTD XHTML 1.0 Strict//EN"
"http://www.w3.org/TR/xhtml1/DTD/xhtml1-strict.dtd">
<html xmlns="http://www.w3.org/1999/xhtml">
<head>
<title>Strict Document Sample</title>

</head>
<body>


</body>
</html>
```

LISTING 1.5   FRAMESET IN XHTML 1.0

```
<?xml version="1.0"?>
<!DOCTYPE html PUBLIC "-//W3C//DTD XHTML 1.0 Frameset//EN"
"DTD/xhtml1-frameset.dtd">
<html xmlns="http://www.w3.org/1999/xhtml">
<head>
<title>Frameset Document Sample</title>

</head>
<frameset>


</frameset>
</html>
```

Well-Formedness and Syntactical Rules in XHTML 1.0

What about the ways in which XML has influenced HTML's familiar syntax? Several key concepts are inherent to XHTML as a result of XML's influence, but are perhaps significantly different from the way you've been authoring HTML.

First, the concept of *well-formedness* is key. This means that any document that you write must follow the correct order of elements and the correct method of writing those elements. As you probably realize, browsers can forgive your mistakes. So, if you write the following in HTML:

```
<b><i>Welcome to my Web site!</b></i>
```

A browser is likely to display the text as being both bold and italic. However, look at the markup. It opens with the opening bold tag, then the italics tag. But instead of nesting the tags properly, the bold tag is closed first. This is improper nesting and, as a result, the code is considered poorly formed. To be well-formed, the code must be properly ordered:

```
<b><i>Welcome to my Web site!</i></b>
```

This example is a well-formed bit of markup. Well-formedness is a critical concept in XHTML 1.0, and you must get used to following logical order within your documents.

Some other issues related to markup are necessary in XHTML 1.0. They include the following:

- **All elements and attribute names must appear in lowercase letters**— HTML is not case-sensitive. You can write HTML elements and attribute names in lowercase (`<p align="right">`), uppercase (`<P ALIGN="RIGHT">`), or mixed case (`<P aLiGn="right">`). All of them mean the same thing in HTML. But in XHTML, every element and attribute name *must* be lowercase: `<p align="right">`. Note that attribute values (such as "right" in this case, but especially true for case-sensitive filenames in URLs) can be in mixed case.

- **All attribute values must be quoted**—In HTML, you can get away without quoting values. So, you can have the following:

```
<img src="my.gif" height=55 width=65 alt="picture of me">
```

- Some attributes are quoted, some are not. But when writing XHTML, you'll quote all attribute values. There are no exceptions to this:

```
<img src="my.gif" height="55" width="65" alt="picture of me">
```

- **All non-empty elements require end tags, and empty elements must be properly terminated**—A *non-empty* element is an element that can contain content or other elements. A paragraph is non-empty because within the tags exist content. In HTML, you could open a paragraph without closing it. In XHTML 1.0, you must close any non-empty element. Use the following:

```
<p>This text is content within my non-empty paragraph element.</p>
```

Not this:

```
<p>This text is content within my non-empty paragraph element.
```

Another good example of this is the list item element, `<li>` In HTML, you can simply open the list item, and never close it; it's optional. But in XHTML, you must close it. Use this:

```
<li>This is the first item in my list.</li>
```

Not this:

```
<li>This is the first item in my list.
```

Empty elements are those elements that do not contain content. Good examples are breaks, horizontal rules, and images. In the case of empty elements, a termination is required. In XML, and thus in XHTML, this is done by using a slash after the element name, so `<br>` becomes `<br/>`. But due to some browser bugs that will cause pages to render improperly, in XHTML 1.0, you'll add a space before the final slash to ensure the page is readable.

```
<br />
```

Remember that image element just a few paragraphs ago? Well, even with all the attributes quoted, it's not proper XHTML 1.0. Because it's an empty element, it must be terminated accordingly:

```
<img src="my.gif" height="55" width="65" alt="picture of me" />
```

As you can see, the rules here are not so daunting. It just takes a bit of knowledge and precision, and you can easily author documents that are readable by current user agents *and* adhere to the XHTML 1.0 recommendation.

UNDERSTANDING CASCADING STYLE SHEETS

Whether you'll be using HTML, or XML via XHTML, Cascading Style Sheets (CSS) will help you reach your goal of separating document formatting from presentation. Although it's an imperfect methodology, as you'll see throughout the book, the bottom line is that using CSS is also helpful, especially as web site visitors become more sophisticated in their choices of browsers.

As with any web-related language, there are constant changes, additions, and version upgrades. CSS is no exception. Currently, CSS is in version 2 (CSS2). CSS2 became a formal recommendation of the W3C, the organization that set standards for web languages and technologies, in May of 1998. CSS2 builds on CSS1, which has been around since December 1996. But despite CSS's longevity in terms of web years, it has been difficult for web developers to effectively implement. Most web browsers have incomplete support for the recommendation, and this caused great frustration for many developers who want to use CSS as a means of adding style to their pages.

Despite these difficulties, CSS plays a significant role in standard web authoring, and makes plenty of sense from a logical perspective. By separating structure from presentation, a web developer is given tremendous power and flexibility because he or she can quickly and easily apply changes to one—or one thousand—documents at a time.

The Importance of Style Sheets

As you are by now aware, instead of the layout and design language that HTML has become, HTML was originally intended for the basic formatting of hypertext documents. These documents were originally distributed in a text-only environment.

But with the introduction of graphical browsers into the mainstream, (the first was Mosaic, and after that came Netscape and Internet Explorer, among others), the need to present information in a visual way became important. In fact, the explosive growth of the web caused both site visitors and site developers to desire compelling displays.

In order to achieve this, HTML, which was never intended as a language of design, was stretched and manipulated to become one. It's worked to a certain degree. But in the process, developers have been limited in many ways, including the following:

- Inability to use a range of sizing options, such as pixels, picas, inches, and so on.
- Inability to effectively control fonts and spacing.
- Color control is problematic and offers few options in HTML.
- Inability to position text and graphics with greater precision than is available in HTML.

Along with limitations came bloated documents. The reason? In order to add any presentational components to your HTML or XHTML documents, you must use multiple font tags, complex tables, and clear graphics for shims. Listing 1.6 shows a simple HTML document with basic formatting.

In the next example, Listing 1.7, fonts have been added, which subsequently doubled the weight of the document.

To encourage developers to get back to streamlined markup, the concept of separating document presentation from basic formatting became an imperative. The idea was to take anything responsible for making a site visually appealing and put that into a style sheet. What's left is formatting the document itself, and some basic text controls such as paragraphs, breaks, and so on.

LISTING 1.6   HTML DOCUMENT WITH BASIC FORMATTING

```
<html>
<head>
     <title>King Lear: Act 2, Scene 1</title>
</head>

<body>

<h1>Edmund</h1>

<p>The duke be here to-night? The better! best!
This weaves itself perforce into my business.
My father hath set guard to take my brother;
And I have one thing, of a queasy question,
Which I must act: briefness and fortune, work!
Brother, a word; descend: brother, I say!</p>

<p>Enter EDGAR</p>

<p>My father watches: O sir, fly this place;
Intelligence is given where you are hid;
You have now the good advantage of the night:
Have you not spoken 'gainst the Duke of Cornwall?
He's coming hither: now, i' the night, i' the haste,
And Regan with him: have you nothing said
Upon his party 'gainst the Duke of Albany?
Advise yourself.</p>

</body>
</html>
```

LISTING 1.7   THE BASIC DOCUMENT WITH ADDED FONTS

```
<html>
<head>
     <title>King Lear: Act 2, Scene 1</title>
</head>

<body bgcolor="#000000">

<h1><font face="arial, helvetica, sans-serif"
color="#FFFFCC">Edmund</font></h1>

<p><font face="garamond, times, serif" size="4" color="#CCFFFF">
The duke be here to-night? The better! best!
This weaves itself perforce into my business.
My father hath set guard to take my brother;
And I have one thing, of a queasy question,
Which I must act: briefness and fortune, work!
Brother, a word; descend: brother, I say!</font></p>

<p><font face="arial, helvetica, sans-serif" color="#FFFFCC">
Enter EDGAR</font></p>

<p><font face="garamond, times, serif" size="4" color="#CCFFFF">
My father watches: O sir, fly this place;
Intelligence is given where you are hid;
You have now the good advantage of the night:
Have you not spoken 'gainst the Duke of Cornwall?
He's coming hither: now, i' the night, i' the haste,
And Regan with him: have you nothing said
Upon his party 'gainst the Duke of Albany?
Advise yourself.</font></p>

</body>
</html>
```

Another advantage of style sheets: You get a more sophisticated level of control over your documents. Whether it's one document or one thousand, you can make changes to the presentation of those documents by using a single style sheet. Then you simply change that style sheet, and all of those documents accept the changes.

If all this sounds exciting, it should. But the problem still remains that browsers are limited in their style support—this is especially true in terms of positioning. As a result, you will most likely avoid style sheets for positioning elements, and the CSS you do employ must be applied carefully and tested for *graceful degradation*. In other words, if you're using style sheets, you must first test your pages in a wide range of browsers and versions until you get the results you want. You should also take a look at your page without style sheets enabled. Does it work? If it does, you're in business.

13

Note: Many people began to use JavaScript routing to solve the problem of interoperability between browsers and platforms. Testing the DOM version of a requesting browser allows the web developer to create several versions of the site—those using style, those not, and so on. However, this method does have a few problems. First, some people have scripting turned off. Second—and this is perhaps more opinion than fact—the more I work with style and clean markup, the more opportunities I see to create enigmatic designs that are, in fact, completely interoperable. Maybe they don't look as pretty on older browsers, but they work. However, because JavaScript routing is a valid and widespread technique, you will see cases in this book where it is put to use.

Although using CSS might mean more initial work for you, as you'll soon see, the use of style can put tons of control in your hands. That's something that pays off in the long run.

Style Terms

An entire vocabulary is linked to style sheets, so naturally, it's important to familiarize yourself with some of the terminology:

- **Document**—Your HTML or XHTML document.
- **Style sheet**—The style that's applied inside or outside a given document.
- **Presentation**—The look of a page.
- **Document format**—The structure of a document.
- **Style relationships**—The way in which style components act with each other.
- **Style sheet options**—The various kinds of available style sheets.
- **Style sheet syntax**—The grammar of style.

Knowing these terms enables you to communicate clearly with others about style (and it'll be easier for you to understand this book).

Understanding the Cascade

A critical aspect of CSS relationships is the *cascade*. The cascade is the concept that there is an order of importance in style sheets. This allows you to create multiple style sheets and, in turn, gain a great deal of control over a document.

The order of importance is as follows:

1. **Inline styles**—Styles that are written directly within HTML. They override all other style sheets in the cascade.

2. **Embedded styles**—A style sheet that appears in the head portion of an HTML document and controls that document. It overrides any style other than inline user-defined.

3. **Linked styles**—An external sheet.

4. **Imported styles**— A style sheet that is called upon by another style sheet. Note that this does not work in some browsers.

5. **Browser defaults**—Any settings within a browser. The browser defaults appear only when no style is available or when a browser does not properly interpret a given style.

Another type of style sheet that is used infrequently but overrides all other styles in a cascade are *user-defined* style sheets. You or I can write these style sheets and set them up in a browser to override the style of any page viewed.

CSS Relationships

The concept of a style sheet is not a new one. In fact, it comes from the world of print, where style sheets are employed to control layout and presentation in a variety of applications. The relationship of a style sheet to the document(s) it controls is an important one—one that bears study before diving in. There are also relationships within style documents themselves, with a specific hierarchy of rules that apply to specific elements.

As within a human family, these relationships are highly structured. They're necessary for style to work properly and for you to gain control of your HTML documents effectively. The most overt relationships in style are parent–child relationships.

A *parent* is an element that is higher up in the markup hierarchy than another element. For example, <body> is the parent to <p> (among other elements). In this example, the paragraph symbol is the *child*. Of course, a child can also be a parent—just as in real life. *Siblings* also exist. These elements are children to one given parent.

Inheritance in Detail

As within families, features can be inherited. For example, a child might have the same hair or eye color as one of his parents. In CSS, children can inherit the features of their parents. If I want my `body` element to have a font size of 10 and a blue color, unless I specifically write a rule that gives a child other presentation features, all the children will have a font size of 10 and a blue color. But if I declare that all headers level 1 (`h1`) are to be size 12 with a red color, `h1` elements will be size 12 and red, but all the other children remain size 10 and blue until I add another rule. Say that I declare my `h2` value as green, but I don't state a size. All `h2` values will be green, and the size will be 10 because `h2` inherits the size feature from its parent rather than sibling `h1`.

It's important to note that not all properties in CSS can be inherited, and certain browsers do not interpret inheritance properly.

> **Note:** For more information on CSS and inheritance, visit Eric A. Meyer's excellent style sheet reference guide at WebReview.com (`http://style.webreview.com/`). You might also want to look at the W3C's style resources, which can be found at `http://www.w3.org/Style/CSS/`.

Style Options in Detail

I briefly introduced the main style options when the cascade was discussed. In this section, I look at these style options in greater detail; this time, the emphasis is on the employment of style rather than its internal relationships.

The following options are in style:

1. **Inline styles**—Inline styles are written directly into an HTML (or another markup) page. An inline style controls a single character, a line, or short areas on that page itself. It has the dominant role in the cascade because it overrides all other style options that might coexist.

2. **Embedded styles**—An embedded style sheet appears in the `HEAD` portion of an HTML document and controls that document. It overrides any style except the inline style.

3. **Linked styles**—An external sheet. Any page that is to be influenced by the styles in a linked sheet must be linked to that sheet. This is done in the `head` of a document. After that link relationship exists, all pages linked to the sheet can be modified by making modifications to the style sheet rather than directly to the individual pages. Linked styles are powerful because they enable developers to easily control many documents . In the cascade, inline and embedded sheets override a linked sheet.

4. **Imported styles**—A style sheet that calls on another style sheet. If you think that imported styles work like linked styles, you're correct. However, imported style must appear within a style element or within an external style sheet.

5. **Browser defaults**—Any settings within a browser. The browser defaults appear only when no style is available or when a browser does not properly interpret a given style.

Because browser defaults are not really a style sheet per se and because the use of imported sheets is a more-advanced technique, I'm going to set them both aside and focus on the types of sheets that you'll most often use to add style to your page or web site.

Inline Style

Because it resides directly in the HTML `body`, inline style works differently than embedded and linked styles. Say that you have a page with content and you want to modify that content at the character, line, or division level.

To do so, you can use any existing HTML element and add the `style` attribute to it, with a style rule as its value. Suppose you have a paragraph that you want to give a completely different style than another paragraph on that page. Here's what you do to add inline style to that paragraph:

```
<p style="color: blue;">This paragraph will now appear in blue</p>
```

Remember that inline style overrides any other style (except user-defined). So even if you're using another sheet that says all your paragraphs should be pink, this particular paragraph appears in blue.

What happens when you want to change a single character or a single line of information? In that case, you can use the span element along with the style attribute and rule. Here's a standard paragraph with span:

```
<p>My name is <span style="color: red;">Molly E. Holzschlag</span> and I
am the author of numerous books on Web design.</p>
```

My name now appears in red, no matter what other styles are written for the paragraph.

Sometimes, you might want to have style affect longer sections of a page. Say that you have three paragraphs and you want them all to have a different style than the rest of the page. In this case, you can use the div (division) element, which applies the style to the entire division it contains (see Listing 1.8).

It's important to note that span is used for character and line control because it adds no additional spaces or breaks. The div element can add a break depending on the browser that interprets it. As such, use span for tightly controlled areas and div for larger sections.

Embedded Style

Embedded style is embedded into the head portion of a page. It uses the style element to denote the section where style information begins and ends. Here's a closer look at the basic structure of an HTML document:

```
<html>
<head>
<title>My Stylin' Page</title>
</head>

<body>

</body>
</html>
```

You can add the style tags as follows:

```
<html>
<head>
<title>My Stylin' Page</title>

<style>
```

```
</style>
</head>
<body>

</body>
</html>
```

Then you can write the style rules that you want to have control the document. Remember the cascade relationships: If you already have inline style on the page, that style overrides any embedded style that conflicts with it.

If you create an embedded sheet, such as the one found in Listing 1.9, and you have an inline style for an h1 somewhere in the document that has a different face and color associated with it, that inline style overrides this one. But, any other h1 elements that have no inline styles declared take the embedded presentational information instead.

LISTING 1.8   USING THE DIV ELEMENT

```
<div style="color: yellow;">
        <p>This is my first paragraph</p>

        <p>This is my second paragraph</p>

        <p>This is my third paragraph</p>
</div>
```

LISTING 1.9   EMBEDDED STYLE

```
<style>


h1 {

        font-face: arial, helvetica, sans-serif;
        color: blue;

}


</style>
```

Note that this embedded style sheet contains only one rule. Many style authors use comment tags around their style rules. This assists older browsers that might try to interpret style in the body rather than in the head. Most common browsers above 3.0 versions, however, do not have this difficulty. In fact, I found that using the comment tags can cause style to not display properly. If you desire to use HTML comment tags to hide your styles from older browsers, Listing 1.10 shows you how to do it.

Similarly, if you are interested in adding comments to your style sheets, Listing 1.11 shows you the way.

Now it's time to move onward to linked style!

LISTING 1.10   USING COMMENT TAGS

```
<style>
<!-- style rules commented out for old browsers

h1 {
        font-face: arial, helvetica, sans-serif;
        color: blue;
}
 -->
</style>
```

LISTING 1.11   A STYLE SHEET WITH COMMENTS

```
<style>

h1 {
        font-face: arial, helvetica, sans-serif;
        color: blue;
}
/* sets h1 style to sans-serif blue font */
</style>
```

Linked Style Sheets

As I mentioned earlier, linked style sheets are powerful because a single sheet can easily control multiple documents. But to tap into this power, you must ensure that your documents are linked to the sheet. First, you learn how to write an external sheet, and then I show you how to link a document to that sheet.

A linked style sheet is simply an ASCII (text-based) document that contains a list of style rules. It contains no HTML or formatting tags. Essentially, it's similar to the contents found within the style tags in the embedded sheet, but without the tags themselves.

```
h1 {
        font-face: arial, helvetica, sans-serif;
color: blue;}
```

If you saved this single rule as an ASCII file with a .css extension, it constitutes an external sheet. You can have as many rules as you want in a given sheet.

After you create your external sheet, you must link the document(s) that should be influenced by the sheet to the sheet. To do this, add the following element into the head portion of your HTML document:

```
<head>
<title>My Stylin' Page</title>
<link href="stylesheet.css" rel="stylesheet" type="text/css">
</head>
```

Because the link element is empty, in XHTML, you must close it with a trailing slash, as follows:

```
<link href="stylesheet.css" rel="stylesheet" type="text/css" />
```

The link tag links the document to another page. The href attribute is the reference. Be sure to include any path in the attribute value. In this example, the style sheet is in the same directory as the HTML document. However, you might want to structure your directories differently. Just be sure to point to the correct location and name. Name your file anything you want, but be certain it has the .css extension. The `rel` attribute describes the type of relationship the link is implying; in this case, an HTML page to a style sheet. Finally, the `type` attribute value describes the multipurpose internet mail extensions (MIME) type of the file; in this case, `text/css`.

Style Syntax Overview

Earlier in this chapter, I discussed how elements, attributes, and values in HTML, XHTML, and XML are analogous to a sentence when they're put together in a string. Style sheets have a grammar of their own. Although it's somewhat similar to the concepts I've already introduced, style grammar has different nomenclature. In this section, I introduce style-sheet syntax terminology, and I discuss each term in-depth with examples of each.

- **Selector**—Defines which part of the document is to relate to the style. Different kinds of selectors exist, including *simple* and *class* selectors. A simple selector is any element that exists in the document itself. In HTML, this could be a paragraph, header, or link. A class selector is a custom selector—something that you define.
- **Property**—Determines the type of attribute that's being applied, such as color, font, and position. Many style properties exist, and you can find a substantial listing at `style.webreview.com/`.
- **Property value**—The value of a property defines the property. So, if you have a property that is asking for a font, the value defines the name of that font, and so on.
- **Declaration**—A property and property value together.
- **Rule**—A style rule is a selector plus at least one declaration.

Writing style rules also involves some punctuation. The selector is followed by a set of brackets into which each declaration associated with that selector is placed. A colon separates properties from property values, and a semicolon denotes the termination of a declaration before another is written.

Rules are stacked inside a sheet (embedded or linked; see Listing 1.12). In inline styles, the brackets are discarded and the style is written as a value for the `style` attribute.

As you can see, a style sheet can rapidly become a long and complicated document. But remember: It's one that typically resides *externally* from the nice, clean markup you're now writing.

LISTING 1.12 STACKED RULES IN A STYLE SHEET

```
body {

        background-color: #FFFFFF;
        color: #000000;
}

a {

        color: #FF9900;
        text-decoration: none;
}

h1 {

        font-family: arial, helvetica, sans-serif;
        font-size: 14pt;
        color: #FF9900;
}

h2 {

        font-family: arial, helvetica, sans-serif;
        font-size: 12pt;
        color: #99CC00;
}

h3 {

        font-family: arial, helvetica, sans-serif;
        font-size: 14pt;
        text-decoration: underline;
}
```

A Taste of Advanced Concepts: Class and Grouping

CSS is complex at best, and the techniques you learned in this chapter are just foundations upon which to explore further concepts. I've made a point of ensuring that you've gotten the fundamentals: rationale, structure, and syntax. But because of the introductory nature of this chapter and the complexity of the topic, in reality, you've just scratched the surface of style.

But before you move toward project-oriented chapters, I'd like to leave you with two important concepts that will help transition your fundamental CSS knowledge toward a more intermediate level. The two concepts are *class* and *grouping*.

Remember when I briefly mentioned class selectors? You create these custom selectors on an as-needed basis. Unlike simple selectors, they are not intrinsically tied to an element. Class selectors are extremely powerful because you can use them with any element.

Suppose you want to italicize every book title across all of your documents. You can do this by using the `italic` or `emphasize` element, or you can create a class selector.

To create a class selector, you simply use a dot (.) plus a custom name for the selector. Because this style will be applied to book titles, I'm going to call it `booktitle`. My selector now looks like this:

```
.booktitle
```

Use this exactly as you would a simple selector when writing a rule. To apply a class selector, you do have to insert the `class` attribute with the value of the selector into your document. So, inline in my HTML document, I would put the following:

```
<span class="booktitle">title of the book here</span>
```

Why is this better than just using the `italic` or `emphasis` elements? Well, I can add more than one rule, such as making all titles should be italicized and appear in blue. This adds many options for a designer.

Note that you can use the `class` attribute with any element. I chose span in this example because it is the most convenient. But what if you want an entire paragraph to have the qualities ascribed to `.booktitle`? That's easy! Just write it this way:

```
<p class="booktitle"> . . . </p>
```

Your entire paragraph takes on the style declared in your class selector.

Grouping can be described as style shorthand. You can use grouping to streamline your style code. Without grouping, an example of properties and values within a body rule might look like this:

```
body {
        font-family: arial, san-serif;
        font-size: 13pt;
        line-height: 14pt;
        font-weight: bold;
        font- style: normal;
}
```

With grouping, you can simply name the attribute font and stack the arguments, like this:

```
body {
        font: bold normal 13pt/14pt arial, san-serif;
}
```

There's order in grouping. In other words, things must be placed in specific order if you want them to work properly. To exemplify how order in grouping works, you can group margins using the `margin:` property. However, you must follow the property with the top, right, left, and bottom margin values in that order. Be sure to specify all these values when grouping; otherwise, you end up with the same value applied to everything.

```
body {
        margin: .10in .75in .75in .10in;
}
```

You can also group any selectors that you'd like to have the same attributes. For example, if you want to assign certain attributes to headers level 1-3, you can write the following:

```
h1, h2, h3 {
        font: 14pt san-serif;
}
```

Certainly, there's much more to XML, HTML, XHTML, and style sheets. You get to exercise them all in the upcoming chapters.

MORE MAGIC

With the relationship between XML, HTML, XHTML, and CSS clear in your mind, you might appreciate some general tips and guidelines to follow when working to choose and use the best markup for your project.

Choosing Between XML, HTML, and XHTML

Which is the best markup method for you? Well, of course it mostly depends on the project. Most web designers focus on HTML or XHTML to write their markup. Because many companies are committed to HTML and, as of yet, have not considered XHTML, using HTML 4.01 (the last version of HTML) is perfectly acceptable. However, in my experience, adherence to the HTML 4 recommendation is minimal. The renegade that I am, I encourage everyone to use and advocate the use of standard practices: adhering to HTML syntactical rules and validating pages. This way, you stick with the familiar HTML in use and still conform to standardized methods.

Some web developers will be able to use XHTML. At close study, there's really little difference in the DTD's found HTML 4 and XHTML 1.0. So, if you're just starting to write web pages, or have the opportunity to try out XHTML 1.0, do so. I wouldn't, however, recommend changing large sites from HTML to XHTML. The more important issue is to adhere to the standard and validate those documents.

What about XML? For advanced web development applications involving the need to keep data extremely organized, XML comes in handy. But for the web designer, XML itself is not an ideal way to create documents for a web browser or other user agent. However, XML applications, such as SVG, SMIL, or WML, are beginning to have an impact on the way web designers work.

Using Style

How do you best choose a style approach? Here are some ideas to help guide you:

- **If you have a site that requires consistent style applied across the entire site, begin with an external style sheet**—This helps you apply that style consistently and have the power to make changes to the entire site by simply changing the single style sheet document.

- **If you have specialty pages that require unique style features, it's helpful to use an embedded sheet**—You might also want to create a second linked style sheet as an alternative. I like this method because the style entirely stays out of the main document.

- **Use inline style to override existing styles**—Use inline style also when you aren't using style at all anywhere else, but would like to apply a style or two to a given document.

If you have the opportunity to plan in advance how your site will be structured, it's usually easier to see how you can best manage style. Sometimes, however, you'll be redesigning an existing site, which makes undoing past practices somewhat difficult.

Ultimately, the more simplistic you keep your markup and CSS, the better you—and anyone else working with you—will be able to manage pages.

PART II

POPULAR SITES

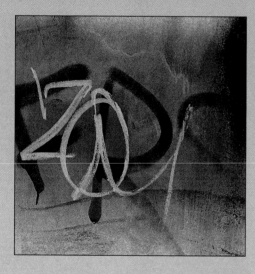

UPDATING A DAILY NEWS SITE

"The job of the news media is to comfort

the afflicted and to afflict the comfortable."

—CHARLES LAUGHTON AS AN ENGLISH
BARRISTER IN *WITNESS FOR THE
PROSECUTION*

Many web sites need updates on a regular basis, and tools, such as Blogger, are only going to contribute to an increase in these sites. No matter what the contents, these sites present the same problem: How can you update them regularly without tying your code in a bigger knot each time? Here's a design that handles updates and archives neatly and simply.

Project 1

Updating a Daily News Site

By Martin L. de Vore

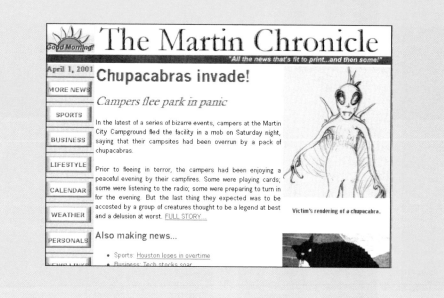

PROJECT SNAPSHOT

The problem: Updating a web site regularly without hopelessly entangling the code; creating an easily updateable web site that doesn't look boring.

This chapter is for anyone putting together a news-oriented web site—whether you're steering the ship on alternative weeklies or responsible for updating a technical-support page with bug fixes.

TECHNICAL SPECS

The following are the technical specs that you need to use to update a daily news site:

- **Markup used**—XHTML 1.0
- *Document type definition* (**DTD**) **used**—Transitional

Here are the additional technologies or skills that you need:

- Familiarity with HTML and *Cascading Style Sheets* (CSS)

- Familiarity with tables
- Familiarity with a text editor, such as Notepad
- Familiarity with a graphics program, such as Paint Shop Pro

Here are the browser considerations:

- Best viewed at 800 × 600 resolution
- Best viewed with Microsoft Internet Explorer 5.5 (Windows or Mac), followed by Opera 5.0 and then Netscape Navigator 6.0 and 4.76

  Browsers render the units differently, which means that you must use absolute point sizes to have congruent appearance under all three browsers.

STRUCTURING THE SITE

The site is structured as a table that consists of three rows and three columns.

The site's architecture is columnar, much like what is found with traditional print paper. This appearance is accomplished by using a table for layout.

CSSs are used both at the document level and inline. Using CSS permits greater control of presentational elements. It also makes the rapid change of the document's appearance possible simply by changing an element's attribute in just one or two places without having to restructure the document to accommodate inline elements.

Constructing an Online News Site

One of the best applications of web technology in the last decade has been news delivery. News sites on the web can be maintained easily, updated constantly, and linked to sites in a dazzling variety of locations, media, and disciplines. On some sites, such as *USA Today*'s online edition, news consumers can actually watch the next-day's print edition evolve.

This immediate delivery of news via the web demands that certain requirements are met, not the least of which is ease of maintenance. Using *The Martin Chronicle* as an example site, this chapter explains how to construct a functional daily news site that you can use as is or easily adapt to various methods of presentation. Along the way, you'll learn many design and coding tips that are based on real-life situations. These tips will enhance the usability of your news site and make constructing it more fun.

Tip: Before you post a news item of any type on the web, make sure that the information is accurate. The number of libel suits filed as a result of online publishing is increasing at an accelerated rate.

USA Today's web site is an excellent example of how an online news site should look. It's timely, visually attractive, informative, and easy to navigate.

Online news sites don't have to be fancy; they just have to provide a forum to post whatever news you feel is important.

How It Works

Part of the challenge of designing and constructing a news-based web site is combining an aesthetically pleasing design with a site architecture that allows ease of content change, even on a daily basis, if needed.

To meet this challenge, the example site uses XHTML 1.0 markup. XHTML 1.0 is similar to HTML 4.01, thus allowing anyone familiar with HTML the opportunity to build a standards-compliant site with minimum difficulty. CSS, tables, horizontal rules, and simple graphics will be incorporated into the site's design.

As for content, that's up to you. But remember, your site's content will be, and should be, its most important attraction to viewers around the web.

Prepare a Site Sketch

The best way to start a project is to prepare a sketch of your site's general layout and to decide what type of content it will feature. This cannot be stressed enough. Content is the most important component of a web site. The best-looking site on the web will wither and die on the electronic vine if it lacks substance. With the rise of new technologies such as wireless, PDAs, and others that don't have the memory available to process huge graphics sites, the information they can find there is what will keep people coming to your site, not the latest visuals.

Presenting the information on your site, however, is important. Before you begin the actual site building, carefully consider the fonts, colors, and layout you plan to use, as well as browser idiosyncrasies. After you make your decisions, stick with them. Media experts point to a variety of studies that they say prove that readers, like familiarity—familiar fonts, layout, and content. You get the picture.

The basic procedure is

1. Decide what fonts you want to use and continue to use those fonts in those same areas.

   Fonts are one of the design areas that need to be standardized for an online news site. Traditionally, (in print) serif fonts are used in newspaper and magazine mastheads, headlines, and copy. Sans serif fonts are used in photo captions or cutlines and section headers or standing heads. However, with the rise of televised news and the advent of the web, sans serif fonts are actually easier to view on electronic media because their letterforms tend to be less busy, more rounded, and easier on the eyes, which tire quickly when looking at a screen. So you might want to consider using a serif font, such as Times, Garamond, Goudy, or New Century, for your site's masthead while employing a sans serif font, such as Verdana or Arial, for the content of the site. Do bear in mind, however, that using sans serif fonts for body text onscreen is not a hard-and-fast rule; in fact, it's still the cause of debate.

   Tip: When you select your fonts, remember that the more common a font is, the more likely your site will be viewed exactly as you designed it. For example, if you choose Times as your primary font, it's likely that just about any browser will correctly display your type in Times. On the other hand, most browsers will not recognize an uncommon font. Using CSS to control your site's presentation gives you great flexibility in terms of selecting alternate fonts.

2. Consider the most-effective color combination for your site.

   For news sites, try to have a light background with dark type. You don't have to use basic black and white, but make sure there's enough contrast between the colors to promote ease of reading. A black background with purple type might seem cool at first, but viewers' eyes will quickly tire of viewing it.

3 Choose the site's general layout.

Two of the most common choices for online news delivery are the *horizontal grid* and the *vertical grid*. A horizontal grid features most of the important design elements arranged in horizontal rows, either as table rows or as horizontal frames. Large amounts of white space common to this version separates the elements and provides the user with a sense of lots of room to navigate the page. The main criticism about horizontal grids is that they prevent the use of large images and, thus, are a bit rigid.

Most online news sites use a vertical grid design. Popular with designers that seek clear delineation of content areas, this type of grid allows the user to make clear distinctions between different features of the site. When you see a web site that features a left column that serves as a table of contents or navigation console, and a right column that houses advertisements with the site's primary content, such as articles or photos, in the middle, that's a vertical grid.

4 Decide whether or not you will be designing your site for a particular browser type.

For example, do you want your site to feature proprietary technologies that can only be viewed by certain browsers, such as Internet Explorer? Do you want your site to be viewable by those using alternative devices, such as PDAs? Designing for specific browser types might not seem like a real issue to consider, but it does affect what markup language you use and even which DTD of that language you use.

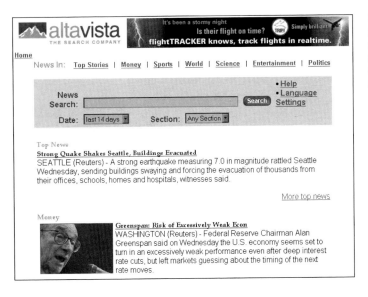

News sites that use a horizontal-grid design feature copious amounts of white space, but it comes at the expense of not being able to use large images.

Sites that use vertical grid design, or a variant of vertical grid design, are without a doubt the most-common format for online news sites.

Note the differences, both subtle and not so subtle, when *The Martin Chronicle* site is viewed in Internet Explorer 5.5, Opera 5.0, and Netscape Navigator 6.0.

5 Consider the issue of accessibility.

You want as many people as possible to be able to access your site. Now is the time to decide whether you want to include coding for people with visual or other impairments, or coding that allows your site to be viewed by non-traditional web technologies, such as hand-held devices or broadcast technologies (such as WebTV).

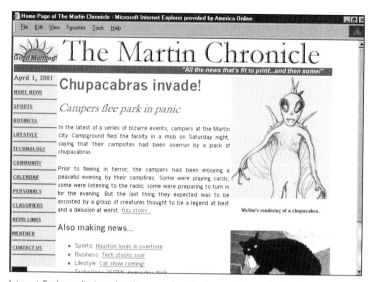

Internet Explorer displays the site very close to the way it was designed to look.

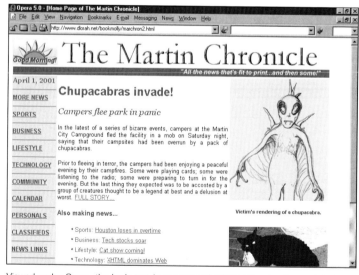

Viewed under Opera, the body text is compressed, which prevents alignment between the elements in the columns. In addition, the horizontal rule is not rendered in color.

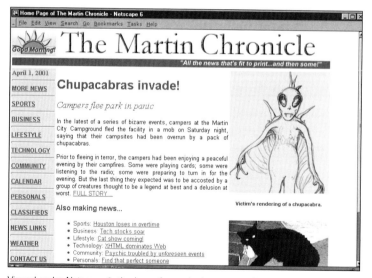

Viewed under Netscape 6, the legs of copy in the center column and the cutlines in the right column are no longer aligned, the text size appears smaller, the leading between the links in the unordered list is smaller, and the horizontal rule isn't displayed in color.

SETTING UP THE DOCUMENT

Ready to build your site and enter the wonderful world of web journalism? Good. Let's start. For this example, we will refer back to *The Martin Chronicle* web page.

To set up your document, follow these steps:

1 Sketch the layout you want to use to display your site.

2 Set up an XHTML 1.0 transitional document shell, as shown here:

```
<?xml version="1.0" encoding="UTF-8"?>

<!DOCTYPE html PUBLIC "-//W3C//DTD XHTML 1.0 Transitional//EN"
"DTD/xhtml1-transitional.dtd">

<html xmlns="http://www.w3.org/1999/xhtml" xml:lang="en" lang="en">



</html>
```

3 Prior to the </html> tag, assemble the head of the document, as shown here:

4 Now put your own information in the meta tags and between the opening and closing title and style tags. This information usually includes the name of the author of the document, keywords associated with the document, and a brief description of the document.

```
<head>

<meta name="author" content="your name" />

<meta name="keywords" content="important keywords that help search engines and robots
index your site" />

<meta name="description" content="A brief description of your site" />

<!-- This is a good place to use an author comment tag to include site revision
information. -->

<title>What the title of this site will be</title>

<style type="text/css">

<!-- Here, you will have either a document level style sheet that applies to this page
only or a linked style sheet saved as a separate file on your server that governs the
styles of all the pages in your site. Although older model browsers are gradually
disappearing, it's still a good idea to comment out your style sheet in case your
document is viewed by a browser that can't handle CSS. -->

</style>



</head>
```

Tip: If your style sheet takes up as much space as this example, it might be better to make it a separate document and link to it, instead of incorporating it at the document level. It works fine either way, but the use of a linked style sheet allows fewer lines of code in the document's head, which makes the source code easier to work with. On the other hand, by including the style sheet in the actual document, changing attributes is easier than having to switch back and forth between two documents.

5 Following the closing head tag </head>, insert the opening and closing body tags:

Save your document at this time. Using a consistent naming convention is helpful if you plan to archive your pages or to have them indexed by search engines. For example, you can incorporate the date of the document in your filename, such as www.themartinchronicle.com/marchron04-01-01.html

```
<body>

</body>
```

IMPLEMENTING THE LAYOUT

Now you have completed a shell of an entire XHTML online news page. But you're probably thinking, "What about the stuff that goes on the page—the articles, photos, and the other stuff that's visible?" It's time to transform that sketch of the site's layout into reality. If the web was a perfect world, you could accomplish the vertical grid layout with CSS. Because various browsers display CSS differently, however, tables are more a reliable method at this time.

1 Immediately following the <body> tag, insert a <table> tag. Insert the closing table tag </table> immediately before the closing </body> tag:

This prepares the page for a table-based design.

```
<body>

<table>

</table>

</body>


</html>
```

2. Consult your sketch to determine the number of rows and columns you need for the table.

The Martin Chronicle layout sketch calls for a vertical grid of three rows and three columns, so you must construct a table template to those specs.

Use a vertical grid design for maximum content containment and easy navigation.

3 Lay down the three rows, as follows:

```
<table>

<tr></tr>

<tr></tr>

<tr></tr>

</table>
```

4 Set the width of the table to 720 pixels by changing the `<table>` line to

```
<table width="720">
```

The width of 720 pixels assumes that most people will be viewing the site at 800 × 600 resolution. If 720 pixels turn out to be too small or too wide, you can always tinker with the width throughout the construction process.

5 In the first row, set up two table data cells by changing the second line of code to

```
<tr>

<td></td>

<td></td>

</tr>
```

The first row's data cells accommodate the site's masthead image and a cheery little welcoming graphic. Why are there three columns and only two objects in that row? The flag, a journalism term also referred to as the "masthead," spans two columns, which you need to indicate by using the `colspan` attribute.

6 Add a `colspan` attribute set to 1 for the first data cell and `colspan = "2"` for the second:

Tip: Remember that, in XHTML, all attributes must be lowercase and within quotation marks.

```
<tr>

<td colspan="1"></td>

<td colspan="2"></td>

</tr>
```

For a closer look at how the code of an actual row will look, view the final source code from *The Martin Chronicle* for the beginning of the table and its first row in Listing 2.1. In addition to the width of the table and the lack of a border, notice that I selected `cellspacing="2"` to provide a bit of a buffer between the table's cells.

Tip: Using `border="0"` creates the video equivalent of newspaper gridsheet gutters that separate the columns without visible lines.

LISTING 2.1   FINAL SOURCE CODE FROM *THE MARTIN CHRONICLE* FOR THE BEGINNING OF THE TABLE AND ITS FIRST ROW

```
<table width="720" cellspacing="2" border="0">

<!-- This top row will be used to display a flag, banner or logo
of the site and perhaps a teaser or link to a permanent weather
or national news site. -->
<tr>

<td style="color: #086848; background-color: #DEF3BD;"
colspan="1" width="100">
<span class="left">
<img src="sun.gif" width="100" height="55" alt="Good Morning!" />
</span></td>

<td colspan="2">
<span class="top">
<img src="marchron.gif" width="599" height="55" alt="Masthead art
of The Martin Chronicle" />
</span></td>


</tr>
```

7 Change the second row of the table to

The second row of *The Martin Chronicle's* table is a single graphic that spans three columns. The `colspan="3"` sets this up.

```
<tr>

<td colspan="3"></td>

</tr>
```

8 For the third row, set up three columns, each of `colspan="1"`, and put the row in place in the table with the rows that you already developed:

The bulk of the site's news content is located in the third row and three distinct columns are needed. This will be the primary content area of the basic shell for your vertical grid daily news site.

Tip: By selecting fixed sizes for your illustrations, fixed sizes for blocks of text, fixed menu categories, and a fixed number of links in the unordered list at the bottom of row three, column two, you can make your site basically a "plug in and go" site. All you have to do is cut and paste your text, change the headlines and links, change the names and `alt` tags for the illustrations, save the new document with a new name or date, and upload it to your server to have a low-maintenance daily news site. And, if the content of your site comes dynamically from a database, this also makes it easy to add dynamic content to your site.

```html
<table width="720">
<tr>

<td colspan="1"></td><td colspan="2"></td>
</tr>

<tr>

<td colspan="3"></td>

</tr>

<tr>

<td colspan="1"></td>

<td colspan="1"></td>

<td colspan="1"></td>

</tr>
</table>
```

CONSTRUCTING THE TABLE OF CONTENTS COLUMN

You've got the basic structure now, but what about the content of the three columns in the third row? As you remember from the layout sketch, the left column of the third row is used for site navigation. How you arrange this on your site is entirely up to you. For content and aesthetics purposes of *The Martin Chronicle*, I included a non-linking date, links to pages that correspond to recognizable sections of news sites, links to other news and weather sites, a link for people to contact me, and a nice graphic at the bottom of the column to provide a little closure and some extra color.

To add the table of contents to the third column

1 Place a comment in the left column with an author comment to tell yourself, and others, to explain the rationale behind the column's construction:

```
<!-- This left column will be used as a table of contents
containing the publication date of this document, links to
specific news pages in the site, and graphics or advertisements
can also be placed in this column following the links to the
sites inside pages. -->
```

2 Start the code with the standard table row (<tr>) tag followed by the open <td> tag and close </td> tag:

```
<tr>

<td colspan="1"></td>

</tr>
```

3 Change the table row tag to

This first column needs to be 100 pixels in width. Because you want the information in all three of the columns in the third row to be aligned, you must use valign="top" to align them to the top of the cell. The column will also have a light-green background. Next, you must add a date at the top of the column.

```
<td width="100" valign="top" style="background-color: #DEF3BD;">
```

4 Add a date to the end of the table row tag:

```
<tr>

<td width="100" valign="top" style="background-color: #DEF3BD;">April 1, 2001</td>

</tr>
```

5 In the style sheet for *The Martin Chronicle*, create a block level tag, `div.left`.

The `div.left` tag ensures that the text in the left column is flush left, dark green for contrast against the light-green background of that column, and bold to emphasize that it's important (for example, a section header (as in this case) or a link to a section). Here's what the style of the column looks like when it's extracted from the entire style sheet:

The table of contents column will have dark green, bold links to sections, which will be a readable contrast to the light-green background color. However, I don't want the publication date to look like the rest of the section links. I want the publication date to stand out, perhaps to be a little larger and even a different font. You fix this in the next step.

```
div.left {


        text-align: left;
        font-weight: bold;
        color: #086848;
        font-size: 10pt;



}
```

6 In the style sheet, create an inline style by using a `<span>` tag:

```
span.date {

        text-align: center;
        font-weight: bold;
        color: #086848;
        font-size: 11pt;
        font-family: serif;
}
```

7 Add the `class` to the document as follows:

Using the `span` tag in this way allows you to apply style to a small section of text. `span` is helpful in that you can use it to apply style to one character or many characters. Unlike `div`, `span` doesn't add any unwanted breaks or spaces.

Now you're ready to add the links to the different sections.

```
<td width="100" valign="top" style="color: #086848; background-color:
#DEF3BD;">
<div class="left"><span class="date">April 1, 2001</span><br />
```

Tip: XHTML requires that nested elements be in correct order. So, make sure that the `<span>` tags are contained inside the `<div>` tags or the document will *not* validate.

8 Separate the first section from the publication date by using a horizontal rule:

```
<tr>
<!-- This left column will be used as a table of contents containing links to
specific news pages in the site. Advertisements can also be placed in this
column following the links to the sites inside pages. -->

<td width="100" valign="top" style="color: #086848; background-color: #DEF3BD;">

<div class="left"><span class="date">April 1, 2001</span><br />
<hr />


<a href="http://www.martinchronicle.com/news/newsindex.html">MORE NEWS</a>
```

9 Continue adding links, including an email link:

The email link enables viewers to contact the site creator or webmaster, which is always a good feature to include on your site.

```
<a href="mailto:editor@martinchronicle.com">CONTACT US</a>
<hr />
```

10 Add a non-linking, 100-pixel-wide graphic at the bottom of the column, and a final <p> tag:

The closing graphic provides some balance. Because this paper was from Martin, Texas, a graphic of a Texas flag seems appropriate.

```
<p>
<span class="center"><img src="flag.gif" width="100" height="65" alt="Texas flag" /></span></p>
```

SPORTS
BUSINESS
LIFESTYLE
TECHNOLOGY
COMMUNITY
CALENDAR
PERSONALS
CLASSIFIEDS
NEWS LINKS
WEATHER
CONTACT US

Campers flee park in panic

In the latest of a series of bizarre events, campers at the Martin City Campground fled the facility in a mob on Saturday night, saying that their campsites had been overrun by a pack of chupacabras.

Prior to fleeing in terror, the campers had been enjoying a peaceful evening by their campfires. Some were playing cards; some were listening to the radio; some were preparing to turn in for the evening. But the last thing they expected was to be accosted by a group of creatures thought to be a legend at best and a delusion at worst. FULL STORY...

Victim's rendering of a chupacabra.

Also making news...

- Sports: Houston loses in overtime
- Business: Tech stocks soar
- Lifestyle: Cat show coming!
- Technology: XHTML dominates Web
- Community: Psychic troubled by unforeseen events
- Personals: Find that perfect someone
- News Links: Links to CNN, BBC and others
- Weather: Links to Accuweather and The Weather Channel

Cats from all over will be competing at the Charity Cat Show this weekend.

Use a small graphic at the bottom of the table of contents column to help anchor the page.

11 Close the block-level `div` tag and the table data column:

Because all the content is in place, you can close the `div` tag and data column.

```
</div>
</td>
```

ADDING PRIMARY CONTENT

You're ready to tackle the third row, second column, where the main content of the page will go.

1 Describe the function of the third row, second column with an author comment tag:

```
<!-- This center column will be used to display the main
story of the day along with appropriate links -->
```

2 Set the data cell parameters for this column:

You want the information aligned to the top. Because this will be the column that contains the primary content of the site, make it the widest of the three columns by setting the width at 390 pixels. Add that to the first column that you just completed and the total combined width of the first two columns is 490 pixels. Because the total width of the table, and thus the visible page, is 720 pixels, that leaves 230 pixels for the final column, which will contain photos or graphics. Remember this number because you will refer to it later.

```
<td width="390" valign="top">
```

3 Set up the CSS to declare the headers:

As with HTML 4.01, XHTML 1.0 uses the traditional headers that you're familiar with: <h1>, <h2>, <h3>, <h4>, <h5>, <h6>. By using CSS, you can customize these headers for use as newspaper-style headlines.

Note: The <h4> header has been styled for photo captions or cutlines.

```
h1 {
        text-align: left;
        font-weight: bold;
        color: #086848;
        background-color: transparent;
        font-family: sans-serif;
}

h2 {
        text-align: left;
        font-weight: normal;
        color: #086848;
        background-color: transparent;
        font-style: italic;
        font-family: serif;
}

h3 {
        text-align: left;
        font-weight: bold;
        color: #086848;
        background-color: transparent;
        font-family: sans-serif;
}

h4 {
        text-align: center;
        font-weight: bold;
        color: #086848;
        background-color: transparent;
        font-family: sans-serif;
        font-size: 8pt;
}
```

4 Start filling in the contents for the headers:

5 Add your main story within the paragraph <p> and close paragraph </p> tags.

You can write your primary content in advance and paste it into this section, or you can write it as you go. The choice is yours. Remember, the <p> tag works the same in XHTML 1.0 as it did in HTML 4.01, but you must close the tag at the end of the paragraph with </p>.

```
<h1>Chupacabras invade!</h1>
<!-- Secondary headline follows: -->
<h2>Campers flee park in panic</h2>
```

Tip: At news sites, it is common to use a primary headline to grab the viewer's attention in combination with a secondary headline that provides additional information.

Again, it's possible to enhance your control of your document's presentation by using CSS to assign values to the paragraph tag's attributes.

6 Render the CSS for the paragraph tags:

This allows you to require that the document displays justified, black, and sans-serif text against a white background.

As you've seen it, *The Martin Chronicle* site uses this design to good effect.

Tip: Do *not* put the entire article in the second column if it's more than two paragraphs long. Use a link and continue the story on another page.

```
p {
        color: #000000;
        background-color: #FFFFFF;
        font-size: 10pt;
        font-family: sans-serif;
        text-align: justify;

}
```

7 Add additional content by making an unordered list that contains links to some, but not all, of the sections listed in the table of contents column, and annotating that list with stories that appear in listed sections:

That was just an ordinary unordered list that you've probably used in HTML 4.01. The key is to remember to close the list items, `</li>`, because you are building your site in XHTML 1.0.

The site now has a main section that features the primary story or article and a list of other stories that viewers can access.

```
<h3>Also making news...</h3>

<ul>

<li>Sports: <a href="http://www.martinchronicle.com/sports/houston.html">Houston loses
in overtime</a></li>

<li>Business: <a href="http://www.martinchronicle.com/business/techstocks.html">Tech
stocks soar</a></li>

<li>Lifestyle: <a href="http://www.martinchronicle.com/lifestyle/catshow.html">Cat show
coming!</a></li>

<li>Technology: <a href="http://www.martinchronicle.com/technology/xhtml.html">XHTML
dominates Web</a></li>

<li>Community: <a href="http://www.martinchronicle.com/community/psychic.html">Psychic
troubled by unforeseen events</a></li>

<li>Personals: <a href="http://www.martinchronicle.com/personals/romance.html">Find that
perfect someone</a></li>

<li>News Links: <a href="http://www.martinchronicle.com/newslinks/news.html">Links to
CNN, BBC and others</a></li>

<li>Weather: <a href="http://www.martinchronicle.com/weatherlinks/weather.html">Links to
Accuweather and The Weather Channel</a></li>


</ul>
```

8 Close this table data cell (but not the table row):

```
</td>
```

COMPLETING THE TABLE

You're now ready to build the third column, the right column, of the third row, and thus complete the table and the site. This column will contain the graphics, photos, or artwork and their accompanying captions. By placing your graphics in the right column of the page, it visually balances the table of contents and its graphics that are in the left column. For a site of this type, one large graphic and one smaller graphic is all that you would want in the right column. The captions of these graphics should align with the bottoms of the two main articles in the center column to achieve symmetry.

1 Set the width of the third and final column in this row at 226 pixels and align the content to the top of the column:

```
<td width="226" valign="top">
```

A width of 226 results in a total of 716 pixels. Because the table width was 720 pixels, that leaves a remaining 4 pixels of cell padding.

2 Insert your images by using a standard `image` tag with the XHTML-mandated empty tag marker (/) at the end.

```
<img src="chupacabra.gif" width="225" height="267" border="0" alt="Drawing of
a chupacabra." />
```

This is what the code will look like for the top image in the right column:

3 Close out the bottom of the screen by adding a horizontal rule after the completed table:

```
<hr />
```

Closing the bottom of the screen provides closure to the page.

4 Close out both the table and the document itself:

Remember back at the beginning of this project when you were creating both the document itself and the body of the document? At that point, you added both the body and document closing tags.

That's it! That's all there is to it. Now, it's your turn to create your own news site.

```
<td>
<tr>
<table>

</body>
</html>
```

Tip: Now that you have your site posted on the web, go to the W3C site and validate it. Go to the HTML Validator page. Notice that it also validates XHTML pages. Type the URL of your site. Click the button to activate the Validator. Soon, you see whether or not your XHTML was valid. Any errors are displayed and you can then go back into your code to correct them. Also, while you're using the HTML Validator, you'll see that there is also a CSS Validator. Take advantage of this tool and check your CSS for validity.

MORE MAGIC

Suppose that you don't want to build a web site that's exactly like *The Martin Chronicle*. That's okay. Really. Here are a few ideas for modifications that can help you produce your own unique site:

■ **Create a different look by changing the CSS**—In the document level CSS, you can change the fonts, colors, font sizes, background colors, styles, weights, margins, and many other attributes. For something completely different, flip-flop all the colors. For example, make what's black white; make what's white black, and so on. Flip the font families. Replace sans-serif fonts with serif fonts. Serendipity frequently has its unexpected results.

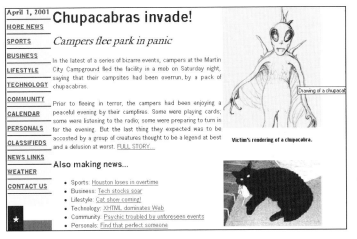

This variant of *The Martin Chronicle* was obtained by manipulating the CSS attributes for the document's background color and text color.

- **Experiment with the actual structure of the table**—Move the table of contents column to the right-hand side of the table. Or, make the design a horizontal grid instead of a vertical grid.

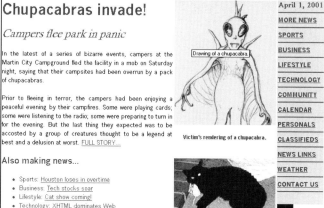

This unusual look, which is actually preferred in some cultures where information flows from right to left, can be obtained by moving the left column containing the table of contents to the position originally held by the right column.

- **Graphically enhance your site by replacing text links with buttons**—Use a graphics program, such as Macromedia Fireworks or Freehand, Adobe Photoshop or Illustrator, or Jasc Paint Shop Pro, to create buttons with flair.

By adding buttons such as these that were created in Paint Shop Pro 7, the table of contents looks more artsy.

- **Link to a site that provides live weather or news feeds and feature it in the first row where your flag is contained**—Frequently, these sites provide you with a custom graphic link set to your specifications in exchange for your advertising their sites.

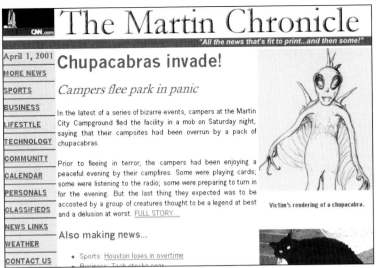

Sites, such as CNN, frequently provide their own graphics to serve as a link to their site.

MANAGING A WEEKLY PUBLICATION

"For a list of all the ways technology has

failed to improve the quality of life,

please press three."

—ALICE KAHN

In Chapter 2, "Updating a Daily News
Site," you put together a daily newspaper.
You learned how to fashion columns and
create readable style. But more magic is
needed to manage the design and technology of publications—especially large
publications and information sites. In this
chapter, you explore some of these
issues through WebReview.com, an award-
winning resource site for web developers
and designers.

Project 2

Managing a Weekly Publication

By Molly E. Holzschlag

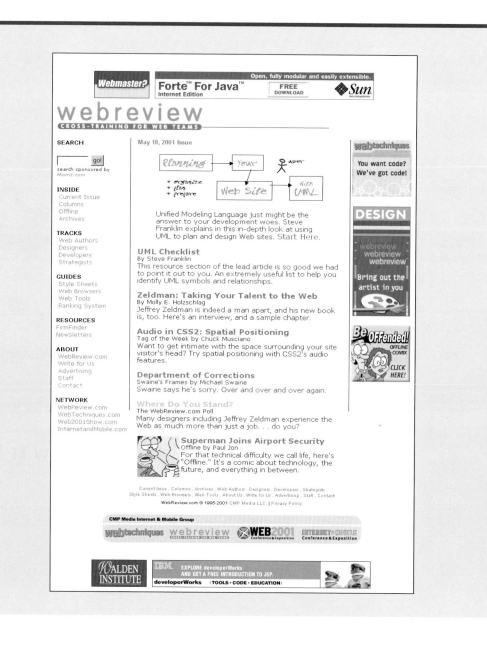

PROJECT SNAPSHOT

The problem: Managing larger, regularly updated, content-rich sites.

This chapter is for anyone who is looking for solutions to manage navigation, presentation, and effective markup of large, content-rich sites.

TECHNICAL SPECS

The following are the technical specifications that you need to manage a weekly publication:

- **Markup used**—XHTML 1.0 (You can also use HTML 4 if you prefer.)

- *Document type definition* (**DTD) used**—Transitional.

From a markup perspective, I used XHTML 1.0 transitional when I developed the site. My rationale for doing so was two-fold. First, a site that's predominantly made up of text conceivably can be simplified to ensure crisp separation of document formatting and presentation, even using complicated tables to ensure the layout remains intact across platforms and browsers. The rationale was a good one, but during the production process, I learned my choice was compromised by the amount of ads I had to design into the site. The more complex a layout becomes, the more difficult it becomes to separate document formatting from presentation.

The second reason I selected XHTML 1.0 was that I wanted to make a statement that showed that XML—in the form of XHTML—could easily be used on the web. I learned some interesting lessons from making the choice to use XHTML, especially in terms of JavaScript, as you see later in this chapter.

Because the exercises in this chapter are comparative, you can choose to use HTML 4 or XHTML 1.0. My only recommendation is that you stick to the transitional DTD to ensure utmost flexibility in a design that's still primarily accessed through the web. If you're shifting toward a publication that appeals to users accessing with wireless and other devices, consider moving to strict markup instead.

Here are the additional technologies or skills that you need:

- Familiarity with HTML.
- Familiarity with a text editor, such as Notepad, SimpleText, or a favorite HTML editor.

Browser considerations: Cross-browser compatible site.

You must use an external style sheet and an embedded style sheet.

Here's how you should structure your site. In the case of WebReview.com, the site uses a hierarchical structure. Top-level pages are used daily. The second tier contains information by year, and the third level contains the individual issues and their dependents by date.

How a real-world site is structured will be determined greatly by individual needs. So if you have a publication site that is updated monthly, you'll have different archival management needs. What's more, you might already be working on a site that has legacy problems with structure and have to make do. See the sidebar, "Structure Inspiration" for some ideas on how to solve structure problems.

STRUCTURE INSPIRATION

A primary concern with any regularly published, content-rich site is how to effectively manage a site's infrastructure. There's no definite answer here—much depends on your publication's specific needs. However, it's a good idea to grab a pen and paper, a great big white board or charting software, such as Visio, and work out the site's physical structure before you attempt to write any of the markup.

A strong physical site structure helps ensure that your markup is more consistent. Where things such as directories for images, media, and style sheets, archived information, and so on, are placed will immediately be reflected in the way you write your internal links. This, in turn, reflects on the markup and the speed at which you can troubleshoot problematic documents.

Unfortunately, many of you will walk into situations that you can't change; pre-existing problems must be dealt with as best as possible. Streamline wherever you can. Cleaner markup that relies on style sheets makes so much sense when it's put into this perspective. Imagine how easy it would be to update a site simply by changing its style sheet and not having to rebuild it from the ground up? Now that's practical.

How It Works

It's just coincidental that I was working on this book when WebReview.com was being restructured. This restructuring meant having to take a hard look at markup and structure. Some of the detailed problems I needed to tackle included the following:

- **Make the most of available screen space**—The old site design was a fixed-width table, centered on the page. Three columns were then within that table. The look was a bit old-fashioned and cramped. The solution? Use dynamic tables.
- **Solve problems with site structure and navigation**—WebReview.com was created in 1995, and as it grew, it became like a ramshackle house—rooms upon rooms with some rooms staring to fall down. The site really needed a

navigation and structure update. To solve this problem, I reorganized the site structure and made the navigation global. I also put the navigation into *Server Side Includes* (SSIs).

- **Manage consistency from page to page more effectively**—Headers were inconsistent in style and color; sometimes, graphics were used instead of text headers; and navigation was incredibly problematic due to the growth of sections. No consistent navigation existed on the site. Style sheets came to the rescue in terms of achieving consistency.

- **Incorporate advertisements effectively into the interface and solve scripting problems**—A major challenge with interface design on a commercial site is how to place numerous ads on a page and still keep the content in focus. What's more, ad delivery often comes from external vendors who serve up their own brand of markup. Correcting problem markup and escaping characters properly when using XHTML helped to successfully address these problems.

Managing issues such as these is standard fare for the professional web designer these days. You must analyze an existing site and make complex decisions that will be matched by equally complex technology solutions.

MANAGING LAYOUT

For this example, you'll use a mixed fixed width and dynamic table layout in XHTML 1.0 transitional that effectively manages navigation, content, and graphics along with a total of seven ads on the page.

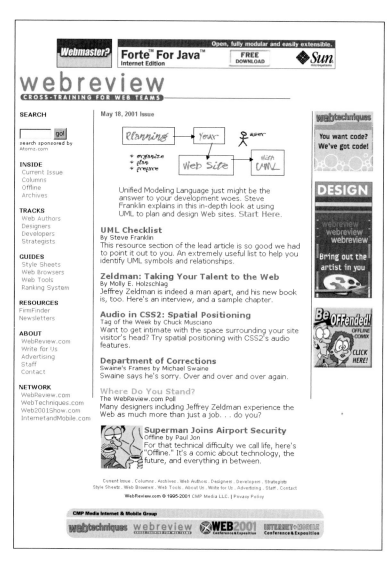

Use a mixed fixed width and dynamic table layout to manage navigation, content, and multiple ads. The `WebReview .com` home page juggles seven ads.

The virtues of the fixed and dynamic layout combinations are numerous, including cross-resolution compatibility, visual control over specific areas of the document, and dynamic flow of specific areas.

Download the code samples related to this chapter from this book's web site and follow along. You will want to have the `master_document.html` and the `table_template.html` documents available.

To achieve a combination of fixed and dynamic layout tables, follow these steps:

1   Open `table_template.html` in your editor.

It should read

2   In the table tag itself, insert the following border, width, and padding attributes:

TABLE CELLS AND SINGLE-PIXEL GIFS

Fixed-table cells require either a graphic of the cell's exact width (such as a header), or a single-pixel GIF shim set to the width of the table to ensure the cell does not collapse.

Graphic shims have been a long-debated issue. The idea of a graphic shim goes right to the heart of the argument that says document formatting and presentation should be separated. If browsers conform to current CSS2 standards, and if all people had browsers that conformed, we could toss the idea of a shim out the window and rely on style-sheet positioning to control presentation instead.

Until then, the shim is the only invisible method to ensure that a fixed cell does not collapse.

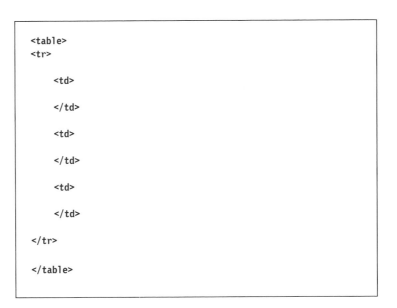

```
<table>
<tr>

    <td>

    </td>

    <td>

    </td>

    <td>

    </td>

</tr>

</table>
```

```
<table border="0" width="100%" cellpadding="0" cellspacing="0">
```

The width is dynamic, set to 100 percent. This ensures that the entire document dynamically adjusts to the available screen space. Setting the defaults of padding and spacing to 0 eliminates any problems with spliced graphics within the table by ensuring that no unwanted gaps appear.

3 In the first table cell, add the following attributes:

You'll notice that this cell has a numeric value, like its `width` attribute. This fixes the size.

```
<td width="200">

</td>
</table>
```

4 In the second table cell, add the following attributes:

In this case, the cell is dynamic—its content stretches to the available resolution. Notice that the value is 100 percent. This means that the content portions of the site will be dynamic to the most-available space.

```
<td width="100%">

</td>
```

5 In the third table cell, add the following attributes:

This cell is fixed. Again, a graphic or shim set to the same width of the cell will be helpful to ensure against collapsing cells.

```
<td width="200">
</td>
```

6 Insert this table into an HTML or XHMTL document template of your own and add content to see how it works.

You can also modify which cells are fixed and which are dynamic—it just depends on on your needs. If you examine `master_document.html`, you see that the main table has additional cells. Play around with the number and type of cells and see what might work the best magic for you. In the figure, I turned on the table borders so you can see the table structure of `WebReview.com`'s home page.

Tip: Here's a trick that many web designers use to assist them during the development of page layouts: Set table borders to a value of 1. This way, the grid is clearly visible and adjustments can be easily made. Switch the borders back to a value of 0 to see the end result.

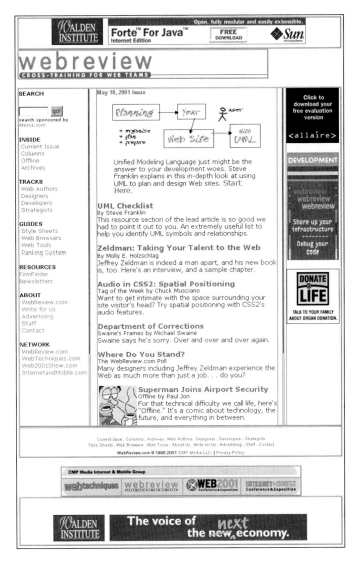

The `WebReview.com` home page with table borders on. This way, you can see each individual cell, the entire table structure, and how the various text and image elements fit into each cell.

ADDING LOOK AND FEEL BY USING *STYLE*

With a developed structure in place, you can now move on to creating a look and feel for your site. At `WebReview.com`, several choices were made regarding the global style for all documents. I wanted `WebReview.com` to have good onscreen readability (characteristics for good onscreen readability are described in Chapter 2).

The bulk of the site uses high contrast: black text on a white background. I also chose sans-serif fonts. I made the choice to use points when sizing fonts (a controversial choice, but I prefer the fixed rather than dynamic results), and I added a variety of features needed for the color palette, link behaviors, and specialty text, such as block quotes and code samples.

To create a style sheet that's suitable for highly readable documents, follow these steps:

1 Download and open the `master_style.css` document to see `WebReview.com`'s sheet for comparison.

2 Begin a new, blank document in your text editor; name it `style.css`.

3 In the document, add the following:

```
p {
        font-size : 11pt;
        font-family : verdana, helvetica, arial, sans-serif;
        font-weight : normal;
        font-style : normal;
        color : #000000;
        line-height : 12pt;
        text-decoration : none;
}
```

4 Add the header and link information.

Listing 3.1 shows the header and link information for WebReview.com.

LISTING 3.1   HEADER AND LINK SETTINGS FOR WEBREVIEW.COM

```
h1 {
        font-size : 15pt;
        font-family : verdana, helvetica, arial, sans-serif;
        font-weight : bold;
        font-style : normal;
        color : #000000;
        text-decoration : none;
}
```

continues

continued

```
h2  {
        font-size : 14pt;
        font-family : verdana, helvetica, arial, sans-serif;
        font-weight : bold;
        font-style : normal;
        color : #000000;
        text-decoration : none;
}


h3  {
        font-size : 13pt;
        font-family : verdana, helvetica, arial, sans-serif;
        font-weight : bold;
        font-style : normal;
        color : #000000;
        text-decoration : none;
}


h4  {
        font-size : 11pt;
        font-family : verdana, helvetica, arial, sans-serif;
        font-weight : bold;
        font-style : normal;
        color : #000000;
        line-height : 11pt;
        text-decoration : none;
}
```

```
a  {
        color: #336699;
        text-decoration : none;
}


a:visited  {
        color: #336699;
        text-decoration : none;
}


a:active  {
        color: #CC9933;
        text-decoration : none;
}


a:hover  {
        color : #FF9933;
}
```

5 To ensure that your list items pick up style in as many browsers as possible, be sure to apply the style to the list types, as follows:

Caution: Netscape 4.x doesn't properly read styles assigned to the list item tag (li). So it's important to apply those styles to the list type (ul, ol, or dl), because Netscape 4.x browsers will then apply the styles more consistently.

```
ul  {
        font-size : 11pt;
        font-family : verdana, helvetica, arial, sans-serif;
        font-weight : normal;
        font-style : normal;
        color : #000000;
        text-decoration : none;
}


ol  {
        font-size : 11pt;
        font-family : verdana, helvetica, arial, sans-serif;
        font-weight : normal;
        font-style : normal;
        color : #000000;
        text-decoration : none;
}


dl  {
        font-size : 11pt;
        font-family : verdana, helvetica, arial, sans-serif;
        font-weight : normal;
        font-style : normal;
        color : #660000;
        line-height : 12pt;
        text-decoration : none;
}
```

6 To add inline code, preformatted text, and block quote text, use the following code:

Remember that any time you require special text features, you can add style rules as needed. The figure shows how preformatted text (used for a number of reasons in HTML and XHTML, but here for denoting code) is now styled on any page linking to this sheet.

```css
pre {
        font-size: 9pt;
        font-family: courier, courier new,
    ➥monospace;
        font-weight: normal;
        font-style: normal;
        color: #660000;
        line-height: 12pt;
        text-decoration: none;
}


code {
        font-size: 9pt;
        font-family: courier, courier new,
    ➥monospace;
        font-weight: normal;
        font-style: normal;
        color: #660000;
        line-height: 12pt;
        text-decoration: none;
}


blockquote  {
        font-size : 11pt;
        font-family : verdana, helvetica,
    ➥arial, sans-serif;
        font-weight : normal;
        font-style : normal;
        color : #000000;
        line-height : 12pt;
        text-decoration : none;
}
```

code style

scrollbar, ready to accept your debugging. You can also just open a window with the `javascript:` protocol directly in the link too. If you use this method, you may want to specify `javascript:void` to ensure your original window does not change. Since I prefer to keep my JavaScript separate from my HTML body as much as possible, I generally use the above function.

```javascript
var myVar = "Three Stooges";
var mysum = 5 + 3;
var myObj = document.button;
debugWindow.document.writeln('');
debugWindow.document.writeln('the value of myVar is '+ myVar + '
');
debugWindow.document.writeln('the value of mysum is ' +mysum+'
');
debugWindow.document.writeln('the value of myObj is '+myObj+'
');
debugWindow.document.writeln('<\/body><\/html>');
```

The line break at the end of each `writeln` statement is to make each statement show up on a separate line. Add meaningful comments to your `writeln` statements to indicate what you are checking for! Also, with any document.write statements, be careful to escape any special characters such as / or quotation marks, by placing a backslash \ in front.

pre style

Within the browser you'll note that code and preformatted text styles now appear in monospace font.

7 Save the file. Link any documents you'd like to have the style sheet influence by adding the following markup to the head section of that document:

```
<link href="style.css" type="text/css" rel="stylesheet" />
```

Tip: You'll want to adjust the href attribute to the proper location within your own directories. When I have only one or two style sheets for a web site, I tend to put them on the top level. When I have more than two or three style sheets, I keep them in a separate style directory.

Tip: To see if your style passes muster, use the W3C's CSS Validator service, available at jigsaw.w3.org/css-validator/.

HEADERS AND LINKS, OH MY!

Briefly mentioned in Chapter 2, there is an historical basis for why headers in HTML are formulated the way that they are. In publishing, the need to designate top-level content from supporting subjects is important. Look, for example, at this chapter. It uses a system of headers that denote this process. If a topic is primary, it received a certain type of header, with specific styles attached. If it is secondary, that header is likely to be smaller and differently styled, and so on.

As you know, h1 headers, by default, will be larger than an h6 header. It's my recommendation that you use headers consistent with the use that was originally intended for them. h1 headers should be larger and perhaps bolder than any lower-level headers you use. You can choose different colors for header levels if you like; it just depends on the aesthetic that you're trying to achieve. What you do not want to do is randomly assign styles to header levels. If you do this, you won't achieve consistent results.

When it comes to links, no hard and fast rules exist. In fact, there's some debate as to the appropriateness of coloring links at all and simply allowing them to remain default colors—blue for standard, purple for visited, and so forth. This argument is based on ideas set forth by various usability specialists, who feel that the consistency across all sites achieved by this is a benefit.

I don't agree. As a designer, matching link colors to the esthetic of your design is important. I will say, however, that keeping your link colors consistent throughout your site is imperative for a professional-looking site.

CONTROLLING TABLE STYLE

In certain instances, such as when information must be accessible through a visible grid system, WebReview.com uses tables for the display of information. In these instances, the requirements for detailed style become necessary. For example, embedded style is an excellent style method choice when you have only a few pages that require the particular style applied to them.

To embed a style sheet, follow these steps:

1 Open an HTML or XHTML document. You can use `master_document.html` if you like.

2 In the `head` portion of the document, insert the opening and closing `style` tags:

```
<style type="text/css">


</style>
```

3 Insert the style rules:

```
td.bighead {
        vertical-align: top;
        background-color: #666699;
        font-family: verdana, helvetica, arial, sans-serif;
        font-size: 1em;
        color: #FFFFFF;
}
```

continues

GUIDES
Style Sheets
Web Browsers
Web Tools
Ranking System

RESOURCES
FirmFinder
Newsletters

ABOUT
WebReview.com
Write for Us
Advertising
Staff
Contact

NETWORK
WebReview.com
WebTechniques.com
Web2001Show.com
InternetandMobile.com

Platform	Browser	java	frames	tables	plug-ins	jscript	CSS	gif89	dhtml	I-frames	XML
Win	MS IE 5.5	JDK 1.1 [1]	y	y[2]	y	1.5 ECMA [3]	CSS2 [4]	y	y[5]	y	p[6]
Win	MS IE 5.0	y	y	y	y	1.3 ECMA	CSS2	y	y	y	p
Win	MS IE 4.0	y	y	y	y	1.2 ECMA	CSS1	y	y	y	n
Win	MS IE 3.0	y	y	y	y	1.0 (k)	p	y	n	y	n
Win	MS IE 2.0	n	n	y	n	n	n	n	n	n	n
Mac	MS IE 5.0	JDK 1.1 [21]	y	y	y	1.3 ECMA	CSS2 [20]	y	y[18]	y	p[19]
Mac	MS IE 4.0	y	y	y	y	1.2 ECMA	CSS1	y	y	y	n
Mac	MS IE 3.0	y	y	y	y	1.0 (k)	p	y	n	y	n
Mac	MS IE 2.0	n	y	y	y	n	n	n	n	n	n
UNIX	MS IE 4.01	y	y	y	y	1.2 ECMA	CSS1	y	y	y	n
Platform	Browser	java	frames	tables	plug-ins	jscript	CSS	gif89	dhtml	I-frames	XML
Win	NN 6	JDK 1.3 [7]	y	y[2]	y	1.5 ECMA [8]	CSS2 [9]	y	y[10]	y[11]	p[12]
Win	NN 4.7/4.5	JDK 1.1	y	y	y	1.3 ECMA	CSS1	y	y	n	n
Win	NN 4	y	y	y	y	1.2	CSS1	y	y	n	n
Win	NN 3.0	y	y	y	y	1.1	n	y	n	n	n
Win	NN 2.0	y	y	y	y	1.0	n	y	n	n	n
Mac	NN 4.7/4.5	JDK 1.1	y	y	y	1.3 ECMA	CSS1	y	y	n	n
Mac	NN 4.06	y	y	y	y	1.2	CSS1	y	y	n	n
Mac	NN 3.0	y	y	y	y	1.1	p	y	n	n	n
Mac	NN 2.0	n	y	y	y	1.0 (k)	n	y	n	n	n

Use specialty tables, such as these on WebReview.com, when you need detailed style.

continued

```
td.head {
        border-color: #333366;
        border-style: solid;
        vertical-align: top;
        background-color: #666699;
        font-family: verdana, helvetica, arial, sans-serif;
        font-size: .8em;
        color: #FFFFFF;
}


td.side {
        border-color: #333366;
        border-style: solid;
        vertical-align: top;
        text-align: center;
        background-color: #DDDDF0;
        font-family: verdana, helvetica, arial, sans-serif;
        font-size: .8em;
        color: #000000;
}

td.yes {
        vertical-align: top;
        background-color: #ff9900;
        font-family: verdana, helvetica, arial, sans-serif;
        font-size: .8em;
        color: #000000;
}
```

```
td.no {
        vertical-align: top;
        background-color: #ffffcc;
        font-family: verdana, helvetica, arial, sans-serif;
        font-size: .8em;
        color: #000000;
}

td.part {
        vertical-align: top;
        background-color: #ffcc33;
        font-family: verdana, helvetica, arial, sans-serif;
        font-size: .8em;
        color: #000000;
}

td.cont {
        border-color: #333366;
        border-style: solid;
        vertical-align: top;
        background-color: #ffffff;
        font-family: verdana, helvetica, arial, sans-serif;
        font-size: .8em;
        color: #000000;
}
```

Note how this sample controls table style. You can have as many style rules as you like. Just be sure not to overburden the document. It's helpful to create a consistent formatting style for your *Cascading Style Sheets* (CSS). Other techniques, such as grouping (which is discussed in Chapter 1 "About Web Markup: XML, HTML, XHTML," can also be used to streamline your documents.

Tip: If the style rules become too long, you might consider creating an external style sheet.

CSS PRINTING FEATURES

Style sheets offer you the ability to hide certain portions of a page. This, in turn, makes it easy to be more printer-friendly—especially in instances like WebReview.com, which uses dynamic, rather than fixed, tables.

Selectors

Property or Value	Windows95/98/NT								Macintosh			
	Nav4	Nav6	IE4	IE5	IE55	Op3	Op4	Op5	Nav4	Nav6	IE45	IE5
5.2.1 Grouping	B	Y	Y	Y	Y	Y	Y	Y	B	Y	Y	Y
x, y, z {decl;}	B	Y	Y	Y	Y	Y	Y	Y	B	Y	Y	Y
5.3 Universal Selector	N	Y	N	Y	Y	Y	Y	Y	N	Y	Y	Y
* {decl;}	N	Y	N	Y	Y	Y	Y	Y	N	Y	Y	Y
{decl;}	N	Y	N	Y	Y	Y	Y	Y	N	Y	Y	Y
5.4 Type Selectors	Y	Y	Y	Y	Y	Y	Y	Y	Y	Y	Y	Y
x {decl;}	Y	Y	Y	Y	Y	Y	Y	Y	Y	Y	Y	Y
5.5 Descendant Selectors	Y	Y	Y	Y	Y	B	Y	Y	B	Y	Y	Y
x y z {decl;}	Y	Y	Y	Y	Y	B	Y	Y	B	Y	Y	Y
5.6 Child Selectors	N	Y	B	N	N	Y	Y	Y	N	Y	N	Y
x > y {decl;}	N	Y	B	N	N	Y	Y	Y	N	Y	N	Y
5.7 Adjacent Sibling Selectors	N	Y	B	B	N	B	Y	Y	N	Y	N	Y
x + y {decl;}	N	Y	B	B	N	B	Y	Y	N	Y	N	Y
5.8.1 Matching attributes and attribute values	N	Y	N	N	N	P	Y		N	Y	N	N

Dynamic tables can pose a printing problem.

The style sheet guide at WebReview.com—written by the *World Wide Web Consortium* (W3C) style sheet working group member Eric Meyer—uses the `display` property along with classes to ensure that certain parts of the page won't print.

To recreate this feature, follow these steps:

1 Open an existing HTML or XHTML document along with the `print_style.css` document found on the web site.

Note: For more information on class and grouping, see Chapter 1.

Use the `display` property to hide some items for easier printing.

2 In the `print_style.css` document, note the class selectors for elements that are to be prevented from printing:

```
table.top-ads, table.bottom-ads, table.footer, td.left-nav *,
td.right-ads *, p.style-nav {display: none;}
```

3 Add the `class` attribute to the tags in question.

Here's a sample from the Style Guide at `WebReview.com`:

```
<td width="125" valign="top" align="right" class="right-ads">
```

4 Choose to embed or link externally to the file and enter the appropriate code.

I choose to link externally, so I entered the following into the `head` portion of my HTML document:

```
<link href="printout.css" type="text/css" rel="stylesheet"
➥media="print"/>
```

Caution: The `display` property is not supported by any 4.0 versions or below of Netscape or Internet Explorer. In this case, you won't be able to print out the printer-friendly version of the page, but the page will print. The `display` property is supported by Internet Explorer 5.*x* and higher on Windows and Macintosh, and Netscape 6.*x* for Windows and Mac. It is also supported by Opera 4.*x* and 5.*x*, and many versions of Mozilla.

MANAGING NAVIGATION AND ADS WITH SERVER-SIDE INCLUDES

Consistent navigation is a key component to making your content accessible. Weighing the various options, I felt that, on a site this large, it might be helpful to pull that navigation out into a SSI. This way, any changes to that navigation can be made to just one file instead of the thousands files that reside on the site.

`WebReview.com` sits on an Apache server using OpenBSD as its OS. On this setup, it's possible to use SSIs to address multiple concerns. With an SSI, you can insert an `include` statement that asks the server to supply a snippet of code in place of the include when the page is served. It's an awesome technology when you're trying to manage large sites.

In the case of `WebReview.com`, SSIs helped me find solutions, such as navigation consistency, easy update access (the navigation SSI is one file and changes made to it apply to the entire site), and a means to separate the advertising markup from our own markup. The ad markup requires regular updating, so it makes sense to use SSIs.

Of course, different servers use different `include` methods. The one `WebReview.com` uses is fairly common. You can check with your hosting service for details. Otherwise, the following method is fairly general.

To view the `include` file, simply open it in an editor.

To better understand an SSI:

Viewing the contents of the `include` file in an editor.

1   Open `master_document.html` and find the navigation section, under the `begin left navigation` comment tag.

It should begin with the following:

```
<!-- begin left navigation -->

<font face="verdana, helvetica, arial, sans-serif"
➥size="2"><b>SEARCH</b></font>
<form method="get" action="/cgi-bin/atomz">
<font face="verdana, helvetica, arial, sans-serif" size="2">
<input type="text" name="q" size="8" value="" /> <input
➥type="submit"
value="go!" /></font>
<br />

<font face="verdana, helvetica, arial, sans-serif" size="-
➥2">search sponsored by<br />
<a href="/cgi-
bin/tracker?SRC=wt_atomz&amp;URL=http://www.atomz.com/go/
➥webreview" target="_new">Atomz.com</a></font>
```

continues

continued

```
</form>
<font face="verdana, helvetica, arial, sans-serif"
➥size="2"><b>INSIDE</b><br
/>
 <a href="/index.shtml">Current Issue</a><br />
 <a href="/columns.shtml">Columns</a><br />
 <a href="/offline/2001/05_18_01.shtml">Offline</a><br />
 <a href="/archives.shtml">Archives</a><br />
<br />
```

2 Compare this to the file master_include.inc.

Notice that the navigation section and the include file contain the exact same markup, including portions of the table that's necessary to make the include fit accordingly into the main document, such as the following:

All the navigation code has been removed from the originating file, and replaced with the include statement, which you see how to do now.

3 Open master_include.shtml, and note the include statement:

This document has the include statements that you'll create and use on your site. The server will then input the markup automatically. When you call up the page and view source, you'll notice that the source displays completely. You don't see the include statements because the server already processed the document.

```
<tr>
<td width="160" valign="top" align="left">
```

```
<!-- #include virtual='/includes/nav.inc' -->
```

Note: Although SSIs are familiar to some readers, others haven't had the opportunity to explore them. It's an old, standard practice that's extremely efficient. As you can see, we were able to create one in a few steps. Yet, the way they work adds much power to the developer by controlling numerous pages with a single file—similar to a style sheet. The main challenge for those readers who want to try out SSIs is this: Be sure that you find out from your server administrator how they are properly achieved on the particular server that you are using. Sometimes, this information is available on your ISP's web site. In some cases, you unfortunately might not have access to include SSIs at all.

MANAGING JAVASCRIPT IN AN XHTML SITE

Perhaps the most frustrating thing about keeping the XHTML 1.0 documents on WebReview.com clean came about when the advertising code was delivered. The ad code is created by an outside source, and like so many professional companies, standards aren't an issue. The HTML they generate doesn't conform to any particular DTD, and they use a combination of Iframes and JavaScript to deliver the ads.

Listing 3.2 shows the markup the ad folk submitted to me.

Taking a quick look at this markup, you can already tell that it doesn't conform to the more rigid rules derived from XML and found in XHTML (See Chapter 1). Furthermore, when you use recommended markup, such as XHTML 1.0 or HTML 4, it creates some concerns. In this case, the problems are two-fold. First, the introduction of any proprietary or ill-used tag or attribute causes the document to be invalid (although it will still likely operate). Second, the introduction of the inline JavaScript that hasn't been escaped also causes the page to be invalid.

When you use JavaScript with XHTML, it's ideal if you can put your JavaScript into a separate document. This only works with scripts that would normally be embedded, however. (Inline scripting is another story.)

In the case of inline scripts, you have to escape special characters in order for the document to validate. The peskiest of these characters is the ampersand (&), which is used frequently in JavaScript. So you'll need to escape it whenever possible.

To escape character entities in JavaScript by hand, follow these steps:

1 Open `master_script.html`, which says the following:

LISTING 3.2   MARKUP FROM AN EXTERNAL SOURCE

```
<IFRAME WIDTH=120 HEIGHT=60 MARGINWIDTH=0 MARGINHEIGHT=0
➥HSPACE=0 VSPACE=0
FRAMEBORDER=0 SCROLLING=no BORDERCOLOR=#000000
➥SRC="http://newads.cmpnet.com/html.ng/
site=webreview
&pagepos=topleftbutton">
<SCRIPT LANGUAGE="JavaScript"
SRC="http://newads.cmpnet.com/
js.ng/Params.richmedia=yes
&site=webreview
&pagepos=topleftbutton">
</SCRIPT>
</IFRAME>
```

```
<iframe width="120" height="60" marginwidth="0"
➥marginheight="0"
frameborder="0" scrolling="no"
src="http://newads.cmpnet.com/html.ng/site=webreview
&pagepos=topleftbutton">
<script type="text/javascript" language="JavaScript"
src="http://newads.cmpnet.com/js.ng/Params.richmedia=yes
&site=webreview
&pagepos=topleftbutton">

</script>
</iframe>
```

2 Open `master_script_escaped.html`, which contains the following:

```
<iframe width="120" height="60" marginwidth="0" marginheight="0"
frameborder="0" scrolling="no"
src="http://newads.cmpnet.com/html.ng/site=webtechniques&amp;
➥pagepos=topleftbutton">
<script type="text/javascript" language="JavaScript"
src="http://newads.cmpnet.com/js.ng/Params.richmedia=yes&amp;
➥site=webtechniques&amp;pagepos=topleftbutton">

</script>
</iframe>
```

3 Manually escape the attributes or use HTML Tidy to escape the character entities.

HTML Tidy is a faster and happier method, so I use the Tidy plug-in to HTML-Kit from Chami. The figure shows the conversion of the `master_script.html` to an escaped version.

Note: HTML Tidy is an excellent tool to test, repair, and convert files. Check it out at **www.w3.org/**. HTML-Kit can be found at **www.chami.com/**.

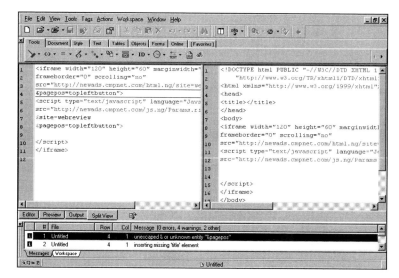

Convert the document by using the HTML Tidy plug-in in HTML-Kit from Chami.

MORE MAGIC

Of course, you might want to make some practical changes to the exercises in this project to incorporate your own style—or to expand your own skill set.

Table Manners

Although I recommend dynamic, or a combination of fixed and dynamic, pages for most of today's contemporary web designs, many people use fixed designs. This is especially true for designers who want tight control out of their graphical layouts.

Here are some tips for keeping fixed tables under control:

- **Set the table tag width to a pixel width that's appropriate for your audience**—At the time of this writing, the most widespread resolution is 800 × 600, with a substantially growing number of individuals using higher resolutions.
- **Ensure that, in the `table` tag you set, the cell spacing and padding attributes to a `0` value**—This helps avoid gapping between table-cell content.
- **Do your math**—Each table cell must have a pixel width that matches its contents appropriately and adds up to the total width found in the table itself.
- **Put the closing `</td>` table cells on the same line as the table-cell contents**—This helps avoid gapping.
- **Place fixed-width layout tables in the center of the page**—This placement helps equalize any white space and avoid "left-heavy" pages.

Following these simple rules helps ensure that your tables are strongly built and attractively displayed to your site visitors.

Style Source

Searching for some style resources to help you learn to use style effectively? Try these:

- `www.w3.org/Style/CSS/`—The W3C style sheets home page.
- `style.webreview.com/`—WebReview.com Style Guide by Eric Meyer is a comprehensive resource that includes browser support comparison charts and style features.

- `www.meyerweb.com/eric/css/references/css1ref.html`—Eric Meyer's CSS1 quick-find W3C property reference for CSS1.
- `www.meyerweb.com/eric/css/references/css2ref.html`—CSS2 quick-find W3C property reference.

These style resources are considered the most authoritative available. Get familiar with them—you'll be glad that you did.

Server-Side Magic

One important way to help in the ever-present need to keep markup clean is to shift some responsibilities to the server. You saw how this can be done using SSIs.

Languages, such as Java, Perl and PHP, and applications, such as ColdFusion, Active Server Pages, and .NET, can work to your benefit by removing certain activities from the client.

A prime example of this is an alternative print method to the CSS2 print method. By using any of these applications (Perl is an extremely popular choice), you can create scripts that enable print processing of pages without having to rely on the HTML layout or CSS markup.

SHOWCASING A
CORPORATE IDENTITY

"You may be a business man or some high degree thief

They may call you Doctor or they may call you Chief

But you're gonna have to serve somebody yes indeed

You're gonna have to serve somebody"

—Bob Dylan

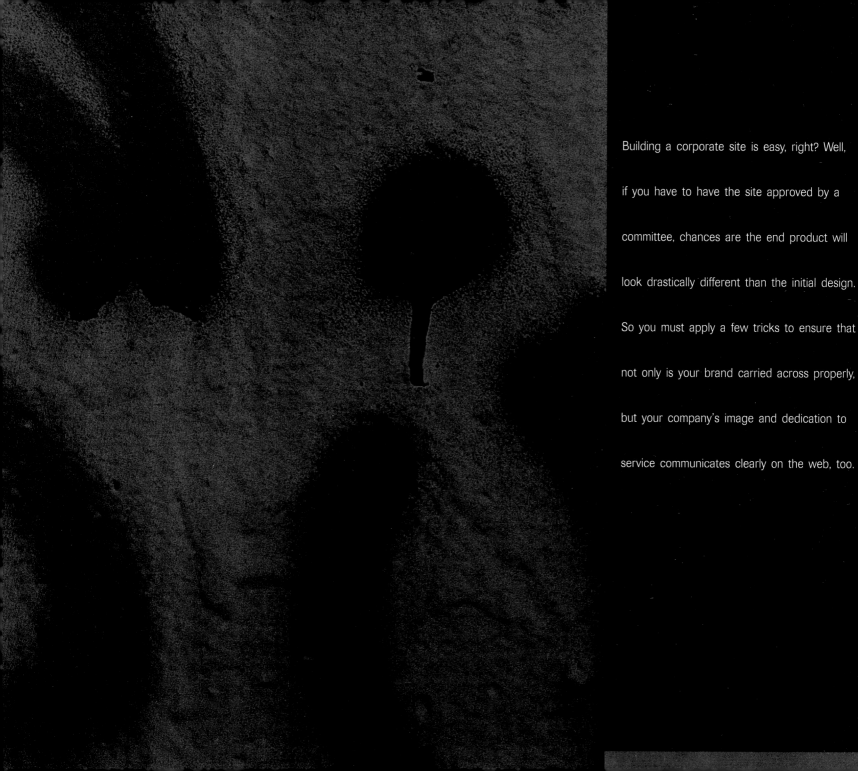

Building a corporate site is easy, right? Well,

if you have to have the site approved by a

committee, chances are the end product will

look drastically different than the initial design.

So you must apply a few tricks to ensure that

not only is your brand carried across properly,

but your company's image and dedication to

service communicates clearly on the web, too.

Project 3

Showcasing a Corporate Identity

By Christopher Schmitt

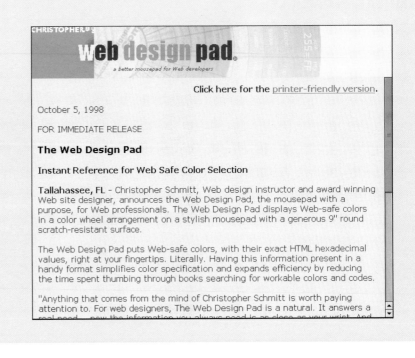

PROJECT SNAPSHOT

The problem: Corporate sites require certain elements to be successful. These elements include consistent placement or use of the corporate or product logo, consistency with colors from page to page, and printable pages for interested clients. Yet many people working on the web haven't had the advantage of a media background and are not necessarily aware of these needs.

The online world can be used to leverage a corporation's relationship with its customers and the press by providing up-to-date, accessible information. This chapter is for anyone who desires to take a corporate site to the web. Here are some unique opportunities to add consistency and intelligence to your site.

TECHNICAL SPECS

The following are the technical specs that you need:

- **Markup used**—HTML 4.01
- *Document type definitions* (**DTDs) used**—Frameset, transitional

In this portion of the project, you step through the building of a frameset-based design for a corporation. Using frames for a site is a personal decision. In this case, I want to ensure that the logo for my product is always present. Using frames makes that easy.

Why two DTDs? Well, to create framed sites that comply with *World Wide Web Consortium* (W3C) recommendations, you must use a frameset DTD for the frameset document, and either a strict or transitional DTD for the internal documents.

Here are the additional technologies or skills that you need:

- Familiarity with HTML
- Familiarity with web graphic production
- Basic familiarity with JavaScript
- Familiarity with a text editor, such as Notepad or SimpleText

Browser considerations: Corporate sites should be accessible to customers and the press. This means that they are ideally developed as cross-browser conscious as possible.

STRUCTURING THE SITE

Simplicity rules the day here. The critical goal with a corporate site is to ensure that information about the corporation can be easily accessed.

How the site's architecture looks: Depending on the needs of your institution, you might end up with an extremely large site. For the purposes of this chapter, you'll hone in on visual and practical elements of a corporate site. This way, whether your site is large or small, the practical ideas can be easily employed, no matter what the scope of your site goals.

You'll use an embedded style sheet for individual pages where you'd like to have style applied.

CREATING THE FRAMESET

HTML 4 was the first place that frame-related elements were officially acknowledged by the W3C within a recommendation—despite the fact that they'd been available in some form or another since Netscape 2.0. The W3C even created a special DTD for frames in HTML 4, which has carried into HTML 4.01, XHTML 1.0, and XHTML 1.1.

Frameset documents are control documents for frames. They set up the rows and/or columns of the frame interface, and allow you to add attributes that modify the way the frames will behave.

To create the frameset for this project, follow these steps:

1 Begin with a basic HTML 4 document:

```
<!DOCTYPE HTML PUBLIC "-//W3C//DTD HTML 4.01 Frameset//EN"
"http://www.w3.org/TR/1999/REC-html401-19991224/frameset.dtd">

<html>

<head>
        <title>Company on the Web</title>
</head>
</html>
```

2 Add the open and closing frameset and frame tags after the closing *head* tag:

It's critical that no body tags appear in a frameset document. One exception to this: A body tag can appear within a special area designated as noframes— see the sidebar, "Accessible Frames," for more details.

```
<frameset rows="101,*">

        <frame>

        <frame>

</frameset>
```

3 Create the `frameset` tag attributes. Set up two rows: Make the top row 101 pixels high, with a * set up for the remainder:

Using the * makes the remaining frame dynamic; it will size to the browser window.

> **Caution:** Setting the `frameborder` and `framespacing` to 0 removes borders from the frame so the results are seamless across browsers. However, this is a workaround and is not part of valid HTML 4.01. It is up to you to determine whether to use this workaround and risk having documents that will not validate.

4 Add the `frame` attributes, including the source where the files reside:

Note that you set the margin heights and widths to 0 in both frames. The top frame will have no scrollbar and cannot be resized. The bottom, dynamic frame allows resizing and sets a scrollbar to appear, should it be needed. Name the individual frames "top" and "content," respectively. These are used later when you add navigation.

5 Save the file as `frameset.html`.

When you create your own framesets, you'll want to work with `frame` and `frameset` attributes to see what features best suit your needs.

```
<frameset rows="101,*" frameborder="0" framespacing="0">

    <frame>

    <frame>

</frameset>
```

```
<frame src="company_logo.html" name="top" marginheight="0"
➥marginwidth="0" scrolling="no" noresize>

<frame src="press_release.html" name="content"
➥marginheight="0" marginwidth="0" scrolling="auto">
```

> **Note:** The attribute `noresize` is a bit unusual. It's a name and value unto itself in HTML 4. However, this changes in XHTML 1.0. See Chapter 7, "Building a Site with Community Feedback," for details.

ACCESSIBLE FRAMES

To make frames accessible to people without frame support or those who might be using adaptive devices to access your information, you'll want to include the `noframes` element.

To do this, open `frameset.html` (or any frameset page you might be working on) and add the following code below the final `frame` tag and before the closing `frameset` tag:

```
<noframes>
<body>

<p>Your site content here.</p>

</body>
</noframes>
```

You can put anything standard that you like in this section. For example, if you'd like to include an entire page of information for display

continued

in a non-frame browser, you can mark it up in this section. You can add attributes to any of the elements that you use within the noframes element, place images—anything you like.

If you're clever about it, you can create an entire navigation set so those individuals without support can get to your site information and completely bypass the frames. Anything within a noframes element is hidden in a frames-based browser. The contents of a noframes element is displayed only to those who don't have the frame support, so noframes is an ideal place to ensure accessibility to your site.

CREATING THE INTERNAL PAGES

Creating the internal pages is simple. You've done it before. You'll create a standard HTML page. This page will be delivered to the top row of the frameset.

Use a transitional DTD rather than a frameset DTD. Frameset DTDs are only used for the frameset, *not* the documents that are delivered to the frame interface.

To create the main page, follow these steps:

1 Make the DOCTYPE declaration:

In this case, you're using the HTML 4.01 transitional DTD.

```
<!DOCTYPE HTML PUBLIC "-//W3C//DTD HTML 4.01 Transitional//EN"
         "http://www.w3.org/TR/1999/REC-html401-19991224/loose.dtd">
```

2 Add the remaining HTML document-format markup:

Note that I set up the body to contain the attributes and values for background color and links.

```
<html>
<head>
<title>Web Design Pad</title>
</head>

<body bgcolor="#FFFFFF" link="#00CC33" vlink="#333333"
➥alink="#00FFCC">

</body>
</html>
```

Tip: Although the trend is to move body attributes, such as background color, background images, text, and links, to style sheets, consider continuing to include these in the body element in HTML and XHTML. Not all browsers handle these features equally. By including the attributes in the body and having them in a style sheet, you give your site visitors the most consistent delivery because style will displayed only in browsers that can read it. For those that cannot read it, the browser will use the body attributes.

3 Add the logo image to the document:

Notice that the height of the image is the same as the height of the top frameset row, which makes for an exact fit.

```
<img src="webdesignpad_header.gif" width="589"
➥height="101" alt="Company Logo Here">
```

4 Save the file as `company_logo.html`.

> **Tip:** I like to make logos larger on the first page of the site. On subsequent pages, I tend to scale back the logo about 20 percent. This is a subtle orientation device—site visitors are still exposed to the logographic brand, but the smaller size indicates that they are on content pages within the site.

5 Create a new page, as shown in Listing 4.1. Save this page as `press_release.html` in the same folder as the frameset and `company_logo.html`.

Create the company logo portion for the top row of the frameset. Here, you're viewing the HTML document without the frame in IE 5.5 for Windows.

View the main page of the site, external from the frameset.

October 5, 1998

FOR IMMEDIATE RELEASE

The Web Design Pad

Instant Reference for Web Safe Color Selection

Tallahassee, FL - Christopher Schmitt, Web design instructor and award winning Web site designer, announces the Web Design Pad, the mousepad with a purpose, for Web professionals. The Web Design Pad displays Web-safe colors in a color wheel arrangement on a stylish mousepad with a generous 9" round scratch-resistant surface.

The Web Design Pad puts Web-safe colors, with their exact HTML hexadecimal values, right at your fingertips. Literally. Having this information present in a handy format simplifies color specification and expands efficiency by reducing the time spent thumbing through books searching for workable colors and codes.

"Anything that comes from the mind of Christopher Schmitt is worth paying attention to. For web designers, The Web Design Pad is a natural. It answers a real need -- now the information you always need is as close as your wrist. And it looks great," says Jeffrey Zeldman, award-winning Web Designer/Writer for the award-winning site www.Zeldman.com and a member of the Steering Committee for the Web Standards Project.

The color wheel format presents colors in an orderly progression enabling the user to visualize the sequence of color balance and harmony. Precise hexadecimal values are printed directly on each of the colors. The RGB=HEX conversion scale is wrapped around the edges of the mousepad. This helps Web developers choose compatible Web-safe colors and reference correct hexadecimal coding instantly.

LISTING 4.1 CREATING THE MARKUP FOR THE MAIN PRESS-RELEASE PAGE

```
<!DOCTYPE HTML PUBLIC "-//W3C//DTD HTML 4.01 Transitional//EN"
        "http://www.w3.org/TR/1999/REC-html401-19991224/loose.dtd">
<html>
<head>
<title>Web Design Pad - Press Release</title>

<p>October 5, 1998</p>


<p>FOR IMMEDIATE RELEASE </p>

<h3>The Web Design Pad </h3>

<h4>Instant Reference for Web Safe Color Selection </h4>

<p><b>Tallahassee, FL -</b> Christopher Schmitt, Web design instructor
and award winning Web site designer, announces the Web Design Pad, the
mousepad with a purpose, for Web professionals. The Web Design Pad
displays Web-safe colors in a color wheel arrangement on a stylish
mousepad with a generous 9" round scratch-resistant surface. </p>

<p>The Web Design Pad puts Web-safe colors, with their exact HTML
hexadecimal values, right at your fingertips. Literally. Having this
information present in a handy format simplifies color specification
and expands efficiency by reducing the time spent thumbing through
books searching for workable colors and codes. </p>

<p>"Anything that comes from the mind of Christopher Schmitt is worth
paying attention to. For web designers, The Web Design Pad is a natural.
It answers a real need — now the information you always need is as
close as your wrist. And it looks great," says Jeffrey Zeldman, award-
winning Web Designer/Writer for the award-winning site www.Zeldman.com
and a member of the Steering Committee for the Web Standards Project.
</p>

<p>The color wheel format presents colors in an orderly progression
enabling the user to visualize the sequence of color balance and
harmony. Precise hexadecimal values are printed directly on each of the
colors. The RGB=HEX conversion scale is wrapped around the edges of the
mousepad. This helps Web developers choose compatible Web-safe colors
and reference correct hexadecimal coding instantly.</p>

<p>You will appreciate the immediate benefits The Web Design Pad offers.
This tool succeeds where others fail by giving the Web developer a
chance to physically see the colors they are choosing, evaluating their
impact when used together and providing the correct hexadecimal codes.
All presented in the same, always handy, resource. </p>

<p>Additional information about this product, order forms, and the
opportunity to view the Web Design Pad on-line are available at
http://web.designpad.com/. The Web Design Pad is priced at $12.95
payable by check or money order. Sorry, no credit cards accepted at
this time. </p>

</body>
</html>
```

Now that you have the document basics needed for your framed site, it's time to add some style.

> **Note:** To learn more about adding additional pages and frame-based navigation, see Chapter 7.

ADDING A SIMPLE STYLE SHEET FOR BRAND CONSISTENCY

You'll create a simple embedded style sheet that you can include in any of the HTML documents to which you'd like to apply the style:

1 In a text editor, open the `corporate_logo.html` file.

2 In the head section of the document, add the open and closing style tags:

I included comment tags that will surround the actual style properties, which ensures that the style information won't display in browsers without support for the `style` element.

```
<style type="text/css">
<!--

-->
</style>
```

3 Add the following properties:

This snippet of code sets the background color, the margins, and the fonts. If Verdana isn't on the user's system, the browser picks Arial, and so on, until a font is chosen that matches the criteria in the *Cascading Style Sheets* (CSS).

```
body    {
            background-color: #99FF00;
            margin: 12px;
            font-family: Verdana, Arial, Myriad, san-serif;
        }
```

4 Add the style sheet to the `press_release.html` document and load the `frameset.html` document into your browser.

Your results should look like the page shown at the beginning of this chapter.

PRINTING FROM FRAMES

Sometimes, people want to print out a press release. If you use frames, allowing people to do this becomes somewhat of a challenge. But there are techniques to work with this:

1 Add this JavaScript in the `head` of your document.

This script defines a function called `printMe`. In the function, the `if` statement determines whether or not the page is in a frameset.

If `window.top`—the top level of the window object—does not equal the page that the script is currently rendering, `window.self`, the condition is passed as true. The expression can then continue to the next statement, the `document.write` statement.

```
<script language="javascript" type="text/javascript">
<!--
function printMe() {
                if (window.top != window.self) {
                        document.write('<A HREF="' +
➥location.href + '" TARGET="_new">Print version</A>');
                }
            }
//-->
</script>
```

77

What happens next? An HTML link is written out that creates a link to the page that is currently executing the JavaScript—`location.href`. The important bit, however, is if the link has a target set to `_new`. This means that, after this link is clicked, the printable version of the page will open in a new window.

MAGIC TARGET NAMES

In frames, a group of special names, preceded by an underscore, are set aside to help manage frame-based navigation. The target is simply added to the link:

```
<a href="new_page.html" target="_new">This page will open in a
new window.</a>
```

The magic target names are as follows:

- **_top**—The link refreshes the entire window with the new page.
- **_self**—A link will load into the current window.
- **_parent**—The frame that contains the window will open the link. You will notice a difference from _top if you use nested framesets in your web sites.
- **_blank**—A new window will pop open with the link. The downside to using this is that a new window will always pop open every time this link is clicked. That's why I prefer using _new, which in some browsers, will open a new window. If other links use this target, they will only load in the new window that has been generated.

2 In the body, place this snippet of JavaScript:

You now have printable pages for your site visitors.

```
<script language="javascript" type="text/javascript">
<!--
printMe();
// -->
</script>
```

MORE MAGIC

Although employing frames enables my corporate site to always have its logo displayed, and using a simple style sheet offers flexibility yet consistency with my brand, other considerations outside of markup are necessary to study when creating a corporate site.

Creating an Effective Press Section

One of these other considerations is the importance of an effective press section for corporate web sites. Having an online media kit gives interested parties access to fast, accurate, and up-to-date information about your company.

For a corporation that's seeking growth, a press section is a strong way to ensure that your web site expresses power, movement, and success. People who don't have time to contact you can directly get the news items, graphics, and any other media that you supply.

Consider including the following information for your press section:

- Press releases
- Contact information for public-relations personnel
- Company location
- Basic company contact information for each department
- Financial information, such as stock values
- High-resolution photos and images of company products and VIPs available for download
- Search (depending on the size of the press section)

Tip: When writing press releases, make sure to include the date for an international audience to reduce confusion. For example, does 11-12-2001 mean November 12, 2001, or December 11, 2001? To ensure that your press release can be easily understood, write out the month; for example, November 12, 2001.

Note: A great article, "Creating an Online Press Room" can be found at www.webreview.com/2000/08_25/webauthors/08_25_00_2.shtml.

Smart Logo Design

Be wary of the following things when you create corporate logos:

- **Avoid swooshes**—Swooshes are extremely popular because they indicate motion and movement. So you'll find lots of swooshes in logos designed for advancing technology companies. However, they have been overused. If you have the luxury of designing a logo from scratch, avoid the swoosh. If your logo has a swoosh, avoid drawing extra attention to it when preparing it for the web.

- **Avoid bevels**—Bevels became popular in the early days of the web. Many designers' goals were to add some dimension to the flat environment of the web page. The main problem with bevels is that they're so overdone (or done poorly) that they're now considered amateurish.

- **Avoid drop shadows**—Drop shadows appeared in web design for the same reason that bevels were so popular. The main goal was to add some dimension to the page. Drop shadows, like bevels, have been overdone.

Now that you know what *not* to do, the next section gives you advice on creating a successful logo design.

Avoid adding swooshes to your logo. (From www.enormicon.com)

CREATING A LOGO IN PHOTOSHOP

Here, you will run through the general steps of creating a logo without falling into some common design traps.

The company needing a logo makeover is Sunflower Seeds, a fictitious venture capital company. Because Sunflower Seeds doesn't sell sunflower seeds, a tagline is needed to describe the type of business so people are not confused when they look for sunflower seeds or venture capital.

The settled text for the logo is "Sunflower Seeds" and "a venture capital company." The next step is to decide on a font. After spending some time at the various type foundries, I settled on two fonts:

1   Open Photoshop (or your preferred image editor) and create a new canvas that is 400 pixels wide × 100 pixels tall.

2   Click the Type tool and set the name of the company by using a script font. Click OK.

I used Lassigue D Mato for the title of the company. It's a script font from T.26 type foundry by Jim Marcus. Use any script font that you have and like.

3   Select the Type tool and set the tag line with a serif or sans-serif font that you have available. Click OK.

I used a font called Mrs. Eaves from Emgire, which is a serif font.

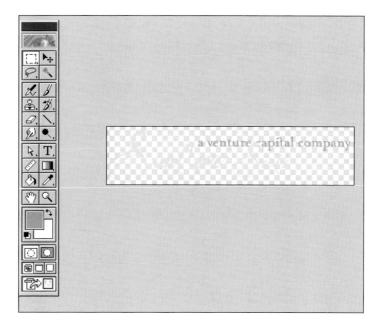

View the logo in Photoshop.

Note: The idea is to present Sunflower Seeds in a free-flowing, personal touch through the script font. At the same time, I incorporate a minor conservative flare with a well-designed serif font. Fonts are extremely expressive, and this is one reason some designers dedicate their entire lives to the study of type. Using type effectively to convey a message takes some practice, but the results are well worth it.

If you want to learn more about type, a wonderful jumping-off place for type can be found at http://desktoppublishing.com/fonts.html. Molly also has a good general article, "Type Fundamentals for Non-Designers" in the January 2001 issue of *Web Techniques*. The article can be found at www.webtechniques.com/archives/2001/01/desi.

4 Position the title and the tagline.

I try putting the tagline below, to the sides, and so on, all in an effort to see what works best. The final decision rests with you—but visual balance and interest is the goal.

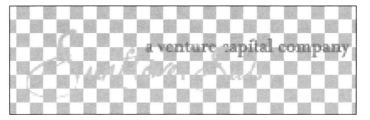

Position the tagline.

> **Tip:** In forming a brand, it's best to use a rectangle shape with the width larger than the height, because it is easier to read.

5 Save your file.

> **Tip:** Create a black-and-white version to be used for faxing or any other collateral material that needs a one-color job.

Just as a photocopy of a photocopy degrades from the original quality, the same can be said with logos for companies. When developing a logo, you must know the rules. In this age of dot-com boom and bust, a slew of companies came online and duplicated all the companies that were online before them.

What's more, a majority of these companies have a logo you would never think of putting on a polo shirt and wearing to casual Friday. When a logo works, it works well. It doesn't speak, but it has a presence. It reflects the name, purpose, and spirit of the company. When a logo does not work, it sends a poor message, or none at all.

SHOWCASING A
VISUAL DESIGN

"I passionately hate the idea of being

with it, I think an artist has always to

be out of step with his time."

—ORSON WELLES

Visual design is a controversial issue among web designers and developers. Why? Well, many purists are adamant that the separation of presentation via style sheets from document formatting occurs. This argument is compelling for several reasons, and a major one is that clean data is more manageable. The other side of the argument is that the web is very visual. The mere fact that we can use the web to show off our visual design skills doesn't mean we should, either. Audience is paramount, and appropriate design comes only after a careful study of both the audience and the site's intent.

Project 4

Showcasing a
Visual Design

By Christopher Schmitt

When the material is, by nature, very visual, such as a gallery site for an artist or photographer, there is a strong justification to use technology to show off the web's visual opportunities.

For this project, you'll set up a simple flipbook to showcase a photographer's web site. Using an HTML page, you will apply a *Cascading Style Sheet* (CSS) design to address the visual concerns. You will also use JavaScript to power the flipbook, transforming markup elements into design elements.

Project Snapshot

The problem: How to display visual design work online without rebuilding a separate page for every image.

This chapter is for web designers and developers who are looking to showcase a digital design portfolio for themselves or clients, photographers with an interest in the web, and visual artists.

Technical Specs

The following lists what specifications you need for this chapter:

- **Markup used**—HTML 4, CSS, and JavaScript
- *Document type definition* **(DTD) used**—HTML 4 transitional

Web designers use a combination of HTML 4, CSS, and JavaScript to achieve a range of visual effects. Some of the burden of visual structure is placed on the shoulders of HTML, but much is provided via style. JavaScript adds the motion and helps focus the spotlight on the visual design at hand.

Here are the additional technologies or skills that you need:

- Familiarity with HTML
- Familiarity with web graphic production
- Basic familiarity with JavaScript
- Familiarity with a text editor, such as Notepad or SimpleText

Browser considerations: You need a standards-compliant browser that can render HTML, JavaScript, and CSS properly. Note that Netscape 4.*x* has limited support for CSS.

STRUCTURING THE SITE

The site structure is in a linear format, moving from the first image to the last image.

How the site's architecture looks: Imagine turning the pages of a book, and reading the information in a specific, logical order. This is a linear architecture.

Incorporating style sheets: The flipbook uses an embedded style sheet.

For a compelling discussion on linearity and site structure, see Molly Holzschlag's article, "Freedom in Structure" in *Web Techniques Magazine* (July 2001). The online version of the article is available at www.webtechniques.com/archives/2001/07/desi/.

SETTING UP THE HTML AND STYLE SHEET

The first phase of the project is to set up the basic HTML for the flipbook. You will need to make space for an image, a title, a description of the image, and links for going backward, forward, or enlarging the image. As you'll see in Step 1, some of the work has been done for you.

1 Download the `flipbook_html` file from the web site area that corresponds with this chapter. Or, you can type the following code into your markup editor:

Even though this is a visual site, I want to make sure that I leave navigation aids for people visiting the site. I added an `ALT` attribute space holder for people surfing without images turned on—or for those individuals who can't see the images. For the links, I made sure to include a `title` attribute. The `title` attribute acts as a way to label that web page. It helps people get oriented within a site. The next step is to apply the design.

Using wrap and scrolling are workarounds and not valid HTML 4. It is up to you to determine whether using them is more important than having your page validate.

```
<!DOCTYPE HTML PUBLIC "-//W3C//DTD HTML 4.01 Transitional//EN"
        "http://www.w3.org/TR/1999/REC-html401-19991224/loose.dtd">
<html>
<head>
<title>My Flipbook</title>
</head>

<body bgcolor="#000000" text="#999966" link="#FFFF00" alink="#FFFF99"
vlink="#999933">

<div align="center">

<a href="back.html" title="back">&lt;</a> <img src="imagefile.jpg" align="middle"
➥alt="Description of image"> <a href="next.html" title="next">&gt;</a><br>

<input value="Remember When I Held Your Head Over the Bowl" type="text" readonly
➥size="50"><br>

<textarea rows="6" cols="24" name="caption" readonly wrap scrolling="no">
Whatever the description, this would be a good place for it. Maybe even an alibi or a
good description of her face. Or was it a "his" face?
</textarea>

<div align="center"><a href="enlarge.html" title="enlarge picture">Enlarge+</a></div>
</div>

</body>
</html>
```

2 Apply the `class` attribute to the `IMG` tag. You'll create the style in the next step.

The `class` attribute is applied to the `IMG` tag in preparation for accepting the styles you'll create in the CSS for this site. I don't apply a `class` attribute to the rest of the tags (`input`, `center`, and `textarea`) because only one of these HTML elements will be used. If you include more `form` elements, you must separate them with a different class. Or, if you want the same style applied to all the elements, do nothing. The CSS will do the rest.

```
<img src="13.jpg" class="image" align="middle" alt="Description of image">
```

3 Place the following style sheet tags and formatting between the head tags.

This creates an embedded style sheet. It's now ready for you to add selectors that will control the presentation of the body, link, alignment, input, and text area portions of forms, and the special class that you've already prepared for, known as `.image`.

Caution: You'll notice that I'm including `comment` tags in the style sheet. This helps prevent the style markup that's displayed by older browsers that might not recognize the `style` element.

```
<style type="text/css">
<!--

body {
}

a     {
}

center    {
}

input    {
}

textarea      {
}

.image   {
}

-->
</style>
```

4 In the body selector, set the background color and declare `color: #996 as` for the color of the page's HTML text. I also added pseudo classes (special subclasses) for active, hover, and visited links:

The old way of incorporating color into a page meant putting particular attributes in the body tag:

```
<body bgcolor="#000000" text="#999966"
➥link="#FFFF00" alink="#FFFF99" vlink="#999933">
```

By moving these visual attributes to the style sheet, effective separation of many common visual attributes from the document formatting itself occurs.

```
body {
     background-color: #000;
     color: #996;
}

A    {
     text-decoration: none;
}

a:link   {
     color: #FF0;
}

a:active, a:hover {
     color: #FF9;
     font-weight: bold;
     }

a:visited    {
     #993;
}
```

For hexadecimal colors, notice that, instead of six numbers, I use only three. Through shorthand hex notation, the browser takes the first digit and simply reproduces it to get the six hexadecimal value. This practice is fairly widespread, but many designers prefer to use the full hexadecimal notation method.

5 Save the updates to the `flipbook.html` file and check it in your browser.

Your pages will have color features as shown in the first figure. The second figure shows the page without CSS. Keep your work handy for the next portion of this project.

Employ style sheets to control background, text, and link colors.

Without CSS, the flipbook pages take on a different look.

CONTROLLING FORM ELEMENTS

With CSS, you can now control how `form` elements look. Previously, people used `font` tags, but CSS opens an entirely new world to the design of forms, including the ability to colorize form fields:

1 Open `flipbook.html` and add the following code:

With the center selector, you're applying `auto` for the margin on the left and right sides of the elements, with a width of 402 pixels. HTML text, or other inline items that are longer than 402 pixels, will be wrapped in the divide.

```
center    {
    margin-left: auto;
    margin-right: auto;
    width: 402px;
}
```

2 Add the following code to your style sheet:

The `input` and `textarea` selectors have similar declarations. Here, you set the widths of the elements to 382 pixels, the background color to black, and the text color to light gray. The margin settings for the top and bottom of each element are a matter of preference. By using `border-style: none`, you get rid of the undesired minor bevels that otherwise appear. For the `input` element, which is where the image title will be placed, I want the text to be bold, so the font weight is set to bold.

```
input     {
          border-style: none;
          width: 382px;
          background-color: #000;
          color: #666;
          margin-top: 1ex;
          margin-bottom: .5ex;
          font-weight: bold;
}

textarea {
          border-style: none;
          width: 382px;
          background-color: #000;
          color: #666;
          margin-top: 0;
          margin-bottom: 1em;
          padding: 0;
}
```

Note: Ems and exs are different than pixels. Em equals the height of the default font size for the browser, and ex is the size of a lowercase x at the default font size. This means that the sizes are set to scale, or proportions, to a user's preferences.

3 Continue adding to the style sheet:

I set a 1 pixel gray border in order to show a subtle frame. Because the border will add a pixel at both the right and left sides, it will make the space that the image takes up a total of 402 pixels—the space

```
.image    {
          border: 1px #666 solid;
          margin-top: 1ex;
          margin-bottom: 0;
}
```

set earlier in the center tag. The thin, neutral border doesn't distract the visitors from the image's content and ensures the background color doesn't "swallow" the image. In short, I want the image to do the visual communicating.

USING JAVASCRIPT TO UPDATE CONTENT

You now have the page to hold your image. You can create copies of the image and then manually link them. That's fine, but human errors could creep in keep during the production process, and you'd ultimately have more pages to maintain. Plus, aren't you wondering why you put the title and description of the images in form elements?

It's time to apply JavaScript to dynamically update the forward/backward links while also taking care of updating the image, title, and description copy:

1 Place name attributes to the form elements and the IMG tag:

You need to tweak the HTML a bit before you can apply the JavaScript. The changes are minor, but crucial. For a JavaScript to "talk" to the HTML elements that compose the web page, it has to know which elements to update. By adding the name element and a unique name for each form area, I can now match up my JavaScript to specific form elements.

```
<center>
<a href="javascript:photoNav('backbutton');"
➥title="back">&lt;</a>
<img src="1.jpg" class="image" align="middle"
➥name="presentation" width="400" height="400"> <br>
<a href="javascript:photoNav('nextbutton');"
➥title="next">&gt;</a> <br>
<form name="pageform">
<input value="TIM AND GABBY" name="pagetitle" type="text"
➥readonly size="50"><br>
<textarea rows="10" cols="24" name="pagecaption" readonly
➥wrap scrolling="no">
        I've slaved for untold hours over indecently
inadequate computers trying to learn things about the that
one doesn't get from classes and books. I have learned (and
continue to learn) by numerous trials and a heavy dosage of
errors on terrible computers.
</textarea>
</form>
</center>
```

Note: You can optimize your JavaScript by indexing the array of elements. For example, if you know how many `form` fields are on the page, you can manipulate it through it's place in an array or group of `form` elements:

`Document.forms[3]`

Instead of

`Document.pageform.pagecaption`

By going with a naming convention, you're free from the risk of `form` elements being added later on and breaking the JavaScript.

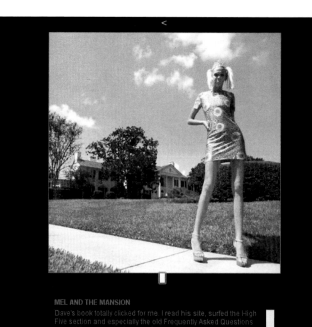

MEL AND THE MANSION
Dave's book totally clicked for me. I read his site, surfed the High Five section and especially the old Frequently Asked Questions page. Where if you looked carefully, you would had noticed that there was a very interesting opportunity to be his intern. There was a catch, of course. You have to send Dave three possible High Five sites.

Add automation via JavaScript to enable a page to have dynamically updated links and information.

2 Place the script in the HEAD of the document below the STYLE:

The first bit of JavaScript sets up the ability for older browsers that don't support true arrays. These are the arrays that will hold the information about your images. The first array, `imgfile`, handles the file-names for the images. The second array deals with the title of the image. I placed the text as all caps. The third array deals with the description of the image.

```
function makeArray() {
  var args = makeArray.arguments;
  for (var i=0; i<args.length; i++) {
    this[i] = args[i];
  }
  this.length = args.length;
}


//image filename
var imgfile = new makeArray
  ("1.jpg",
  "2.jpg",
  "3.jpg",
  "4.jpg",
```

continues

Tip: When placing your images, make sure they have the proper filename extension (.gif for GIFs and .jpg for JPEGs). Also, place each image's information in respective order. In other words, place the information about the first image in the first place of each array.

continued

```
  "5.jpg"
  );


// title
var titles = new makeArray
  ("TIM AND GABBY",
   "C. WOOD IN A RED DRESS",
   "SARAH",
   "H. M. BOYS",
   "MEL AND THE MANSION"
   );

// description
var description = new makeArray
  ("1st",
   "2nd",
   "3rd",
   "4th",
   "5th"
   );
```

3 Add your second image and subsequent images, as outlined in step 2. Then add the following code:

```
thisImage = 0;
urlCt = imgfile.length - 1;
```

This JavaScript resets the marker for the flipbook. When the page is loaded, I set the variable for `thisImage` to `0` and the `urlCt` variable to one less than the length of the information in the array—namely the `imgfile` array. This is needed to inform the script how far it should enable the user to flip through the array, or where to stop.

You set the pieces in place: the style sheet, the HTML elements, the information in JavaScript arrays—not to mention processing your images for delivery on the web. Now you get to the part of the JavaScript that drives the flipbook—the `function`.

4 Set up the `function` called `photoNav`:

Between the parentheses—where the word `navigation` is located—is the name of the parameter. Parameters are used in the function to help it execute properly.

```
function photoNav(navigation)
```

5 Add the following code after the `function` line:

In this bit of code, the script tests the parameter to see if it matches with `backbutton`. If it passes the test and it is in fact the `backbutton` that's activated, the script goes on to check that the variable `thisImage` is correct. Afterward, it updates the image and the content in the `form` fields.

```
if(navigation == "backbutton") {
    if (thisImage > 0) {
      thisImage-;
      document.presentation.src = imgfile[thisImage];
      document.pageform.pagetitle.value = titles[thisImage];
      document.pageform.pagecaption.value = description[thisImage];
    }
```

6 Add the following lines:

```
    }
  } else if (navigation == "nextbutton") {
    if(thisImage < urlCt) {
      thisImage++;
      document.presentation.src = imgfile[thisImage];
      document.pageform.pagetitle.value = titles[thisImage];
      document.pageform.pagecaption.value = description[thisImage];

    }
  }
}
```

If the `nextbutton` is passed, an arrangement similar to backbutton's occurs—but the variable placeholder is incremented by one. Also, if the array goes to the end of an array—either at the beginning or the end—the respective buttons don't work. So you shouldn't get any annoying JavaScript warnings telling you that something's wrong with your script. Listing 5.1 shows the complete `photoNAV` function.

LISTING 5.1   THE JAVASCRIPT PHOTONAV FUNCTION

```
function photoNav(navigation) {
  if(navigation == "backbutton") {
    if (thisImage > 0) {
      thisImage--;

      document.presentation.src = imgfile[thisImage];
      document.pageform.pagetitle.value = titles[thisImage];
```

continues

continued

```
      document.pageform.pagecaption.value = description[thisImage];


    }
  } else if (navigation == "nextbutton") {
    if(thisImage < urlCt) {
      thisImage++;
      document.presentation.src = imgfile[thisImage];
      document.pageform.pagetitle.value = titles[thisImage];
      document.pageform.pagecaption.value = description[thisImage];

    }
  }
}
```

MORE MAGIC

To add a little spice to your site, you can randomize your images. When a user returns to your web site or web page, set the page up to be selected at random for a pool of images. It's a great way to keep a fresh look and add a sense of surprise to the site.

There are two common ways to add randomization to a page:

- **JavaScript**—Numerous scripts can be used for randomization. You can find a useful randomization script with instructions for use at `javascript.internet.com/miscellaneous/random-image.html`.

- *Server Side Includes* **(SSIs)**—Some web servers enable you to randomize images using SSIs. This entails creating a master list in plain text that names each file that you'd like to use in your randomization process. Then you add a command to your web page (see Chapter 3, "Managing a Weekly Publication," for more information on SSIs). Typically, save the final file with an appropriate extension (examples include `.htmlx` or `.shtml`) to indicate the file is using SSIs.

Both approaches are fine, but the SSI process is especially great because it works for site visitors who don't have JavaScript. The difficulty with SSIs is that the methods differ from server to server, so you have to do some research to find out what commands to use.

Card Mania

A terrific way to promote a visually oriented site is to offer free postcards of your images. You probably have sent or received e-cards before. They're widely available at sites, such as `www.egreetings.com` and `www.amazon.com`.

If Perl is installed on your web server and your ISP allows you to use personal CGI scripts, you can create your own e-card service by using the script available at `www.bignosebird.com/carchive/cardcgi.shtml`.

Two excellent examples of using e-cards to showcase and promote visual sites include the popular web artist Heather Champ's creative selection at `www.jezebel.com/stuff/postcard/index.html` and the New York Museum of Modern Art's e-card gallery (`http://moma.e-cards.org`).

DESIGNING A GREAT
PERSONAL SITE

"In the future everyone will be famous

for fifteen minutes."

—ANDY WARHOL

The idea behind a personal site is to be personal. Although this might seem out of place in a book about markup, it is indeed a crucial aspect of a successful and popular personal web site. Many people find that, in order to be interested, they need access to who you are, your character, interests, and passions. In addition, you want your site to have some style. Some personal sites are among the best stuff on the web with design, depth of content, and ease of use on par with major corporate sites. If people get to know you and enjoy your offerings, audiences just might bookmark your site in their lists of favorites.

Designing a Great Personal Site

By Christopher Schmitt

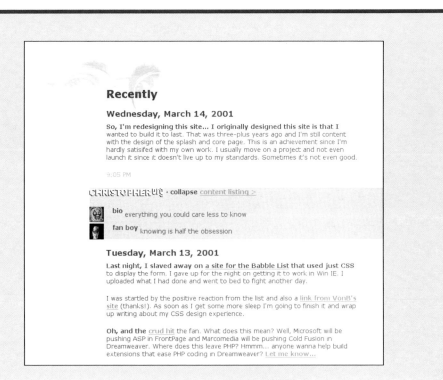

PROJECT SNAPSHOT

The problem: Making a great personal site that's easy to set up and maintain.

This chapter is for everyone!

TECHNICAL SPECS

The following are the technical specifications that you need:

- **Markup used**—HTML 4, JavaScript, and *Cascading Style Sheets* (CSS).

  HTML, JavaScript, and CSS are about as classic a combination as markup can get. In this chapter, I emphasize creating a site that allows for some cross-platform compatibility and creativity.

- ***Document type definition (DTD) used***—HTML 4 transitional

Additional technologies or skills needed:

- Familiarity with HTML
- Basic familiarity with JavaScript
- Basic familiarity with CSS
- Familiarity with a text editor, such as Notepad or SimpleText

Browser considerations: Site visitors will need a standards-compliant browser that can render HTML, JavaScript, and CSS properly.

STRUCTURING THE SITE

The site is structured by using specialty tools with a focus on regular updates. Focusing on accommodating information that is timely is an essential factor in the site plan.

How the site's architecture looks: This site has two main divisions: The first division will be an archive of log entries. The other section is for items such as essays, photos, and other subsections of the personal site that require a different treatment.

SETTING UP BLOGGER

To make the site easy to set up and maintain, you will use Blogger for the backend. A web-based tool, Pyra Labs' Blogger provides the ability to post your words to your web site whenever you have access to a web browser—even a web-enabled PDA. Blogger works by storing your input on its own servers and then publishes them via *File Transfer Protocol* (FTP) to your site. There's nothing to install, no permissions to change, just very simple instructions that anyone with web-hosting and an FTP client can follow.

Use Blogger (www.blogger.com) for your site's backend.

ALL ABOUT WEB LOGS

Web logs, referred to as *blogs*, have taken the web by storm in the last two years. Blogs are online applications that allow web authors to add log features to their web sites that enable the fast updating of pages and take a good amount of work out of your hands. By far, Blogger is the most well known software used for web logs.

Blogger has a fascinating history, which you can read about in detail in numerous articles, some of which I'll include here for your enjoyment. When the Internet economy took a dive in late 2000, the company behind Blogger was severely compromised. At present writing, Blogger is run by one man, Evan Williams, along with the contributions of community members and supportive industry leaders (*Web Techniques* magazine donated a server), which have kept Blogger alive and well for thousands of users. Sometimes, service

continues

You'll need to have a host for your site, and the FTP information in hand. After you have that, the first step is to set up and initiate a Blogger account:

1 Go to www.blogger.com and create an account at Blogger.

2 Set up Blogger with your site's individual requirements for an FTP path. There, you'll be asked to make a variety of choices regarding your Blogs display.

I set my post number on 6, and I turned off archives. You can always turn them back on later.

3 Write five entries so they can be used for testing.

4 Select Post and Publish.

At the end of the publishing sequence, make sure that you have successfully published your site with the test entries.

continued

outages occur, but the service is completely free, and considering it's run by one guy at this point, it's still an awesome thing.

The act of writing a web log is referred to as *blogging*. In many ways, it's a personal and profound use of the web, and reminiscent of the early days of the home page.

To learn more about Blogger, and blogging, check out "Labs, Robots, and Giant Floating Brains: The Amazingly True Story of Blogger!" by the humorous Biz Stone (www.webreview.com/2001/03_09/strategists/index02.shtml). For a more foundational story on blogging in general, see www.webreview.com/2000/07_07/designers/07_07_00_1.shtml.

Start with the Blogger template.

DESIGNING YOUR BLOG

With most online blogs, the paragraphs rest along a grid format. From top to bottom, the entries sit on top of each another.

Avoid bland lists of entries.

Monday, March 26, 2001

First paragraph Content gets displayed here. Lorem ipsum dolor sit amet, consectetaur adipisicing elit, sed do eiusmod tempor incididunt ut labore et dolore magna aliqua. Lorem ipsum dolor sit amet, consectetaur adipisicing elit, sed do eiusmod tempor incididunt ut labore et dolore magna aliqua.

Monday, March 25, 2001

Second entry Content gets displayed here. Lorem ipsum dolor sit amet, consectetaur adipisicing elit, sed do eiusmod tempor incididunt ut labore et dolore magna aliqua. Lorem ipsum dolor sit amet, consectetaur adipisicing elit, sed do eiusmod tempor incididunt ut labore et dolore magna aliqua.

Lorem ipsum dolor sit amet, consectetaur adipisicing elit, sed do eiusmod tempor incididunt ut labore et dolore magna aliqua. Lorem ipsum dolor sit amet, consectetaur adipisicing elit, sed do eiusmod tempor incididunt ut labore et dolore magna aliqua.

Monday, March 24, 2001

Third entry Content gets displayed here. Lorem ipsum dolor sit amet, consectetaur adipisicing elit, sed do eiusmod tempor incididunt ut labore et dolore magna aliqua. Lorem ipsum dolor sit amet, consectetaur adipisicing elit, sed do eiusmod tempor incididunt ut labore et dolore magna aliqua.

Monday, March 23, 2001

Fourth entry Content gets displayed here. Lorem ipsum dolor sit amet, consectetaur adipisicing elit, sed do eiusmod tempor incididunt ut labore et dolore magna aliqua. Lorem ipsum dolor sit amet, consectetaur adipisicing elit, sed do eiusmod tempor incididunt ut labore et dolore magna aliqua.

Fourth entry Content gets displayed here. Lorem ipsum dolor sit amet, consectetaur adipisicing elit, sed do eiusmod tempor incididunt ut labore et dolore magna aliqua. Lorem ipsum dolor sit amet, consectetaur adipisicing elit, sed do eiusmod tempor incididunt ut labore et dolore magna aliqua.

Fourth entry Content gets displayed here. Lorem ipsum dolor sit amet, consectetaur adipisicing elit, sed do eiusmod tempor incididunt ut labore et dolore magna aliqua. Lorem ipsum dolor sit amet, consectetaur adipisicing elit, sed do eiusmod tempor incididunt ut labore et dolore magna aliqua.

To keep your audience happy with witty writings, but make the entries more appealing to the eye, you must visually stagger the blog entries. This is my preference, and it allows for readers' eyes to skim from one entry to another without getting "visually" bored with the layout.

Stagger the entries to add visual interest.

Monday, March 26, 2001

First paragraph Content gets displayed here. Lorem ipsum dolor sit amet, consectetaur adipisicing elit, sed do eiusmod tempor incididunt ut labore et dolore magna aliqua. Lorem ipsum dolor sit amet, consectetaur adipisicing elit, sed do eiusmod tempor incididunt ut labore et dolore magna aliqua.

Monday, March 25, 2001

Second entry Content gets displayed here. Lorem ipsum dolor sit amet, consectetaur adipisicing elit, sed do eiusmod tempor incididunt ut labore et dolore magna aliqua. Lorem ipsum dolor sit amet, consectetaur adipisicing elit, sed do eiusmod tempor incididunt ut labore et dolore magna aliqua.

Lorem ipsum dolor sit amet, consectetaur adipisicing elit, sed do eiusmod tempor incididunt ut labore et dolore magna aliqua. Lorem ipsum dolor sit amet, consectetaur adipisicing elit, sed do eiusmod tempor incididunt ut labore et dolore magna aliqua.

Monday, March 24, 2001

Third entry Content gets displayed here. Lorem ipsum dolor sit amet, consectetaur adipisicing elit, sed do eiusmod tempor incididunt ut labore et dolore magna aliqua. Lorem ipsum dolor sit amet, consectetaur adipisicing elit, sed do eiusmod tempor incididunt ut labore et dolore magna aliqua.

Monday, March 23, 2001

Fourth entry Content gets displayed here. Lorem ipsum dolor sit amet, consectetaur adipisicing elit, sed do eiusmod tempor incididunt ut labore et dolore magna aliqua. Lorem ipsum dolor sit amet, consectetaur adipisicing elit, sed do eiusmod tempor incididunt ut labore et dolore magna aliqua.

Fourth entry Content gets displayed here. Lorem ipsum dolor sit amet, consectetaur adipisicing elit, sed do eiusmod tempor incididunt ut labore et dolore magna aliqua. Lorem ipsum dolor

1 In your HTML editor, add an entry with a headline that includes the date, and one to three paragraphs of text below the heading:

```
<h4>Monday, March 25, 2001</h4>
<p>Second entry Content gets displayed here. Lorem ipsum dolor sit amet, consectetaur
adipisicing elit, sed do eiusmod tempor incididunt ut labore et dolore magna aliqua. Lorem
ipsum dolor sit amet, consectetaur adipisicing elit, sed do eiusmod tempor incididunt ut
labore et dolore magna aliqua.</p>
```

2 Enclose the entry within the `div` tag:

```
<div>
<h4>Monday, March 25, 2001</h4>
<p>Second entry Content gets displayed here.
Lorem ipsum dolor sit amet, consectetaur adipisicing elit, sed do eiusmod tempor incididunt
ut labore et dolore magna aliqua. Lorem ipsum dolor sit amet, consectetaur adipisicing
elit, sed do eiusmod tempor incididunt ut labore et dolore magna aliqua.
</p>
</div>
```

3 Between the `HEAD` tag in the HTML page, write the following style sheet:

This formats each entry to have a margin of 3em. *Em* is a unit that represents the current font size set in the browser. The width of the entries will be 60 percent of the available real estate in the browser. The padding is set to 6em. This has the similar effect as setting the left-hand margin, but padding and margin are different items. Margins deal with the space *around* a block item, like `div`, while padding pertains to the space *inside* a block item.

```
div {
    margin-left:3em;
    width: 60%;
    padding-right: 6em;
    display: inline;
}
```

Note: Knowing whether to use padding or margin in a particular instance is crucial to properly implementing them in future designs.

If a developer wants to apply white space around the text, usually padding or margins will do. For the sake of this example, it's important to put padding on the right and use a margin on the left to achieve the effect that you're after.

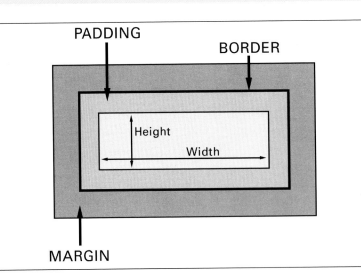

Set margins to 3em and padding to 6em.

4 Apply a style for the p tag:

This spaces out the paragraphs.

```
p    {
     margin-bottom: 1em;
     margin-top: 1em;
}
```

USING JAVASCRIPT WITH BLOGGER

Blogger tends to take an entry format and repeat it in the page for the number of times you predetermine in the settings. You can find this information in the Template section of your blog setup on www.blogger.com.

Here's the standard format of the Blogger template-entry code. You'll add these tags to your template, which resides on blogger.com:

To achieve the effect of staggering entries, you might need some help through JavaScript:

```
<Blogger>
     <BlogDateHeader>
          <h3><$BlogDateHeaderDate$></h3>
     </BlogDateHeader>
          <$BlogItemBody$><br>
          <font size="1">posted by <$BlogItemAuthor$>
<$BlogItemDateTime$></font>
</Blogger>
```

1 In the head of the HTML document, place the following JavaScript under the style sheet:

This piece of JavaScript defines a variable called placement as being 0. The placement variable is a marker for the page while it is being rendered in the browser.

```
<script language="JavaScript" type="text/javascript">
<!--
var placement = 0;
//-->
</script>
```

2 In the HTML file, add the <script> tag to include a JavaScript file (which you complete in the subsequent steps) before each of the starting div containers:

This sets up the area where you'll add the JavaScript necessary to achieve the effect.

```
<script type="text/javascript" language="JavaScript" src="stagger.js">
</script>

<div>
<h4>Monday, March 24, 2001</h4>
<p>Third entry Content gets displayed here.
Lorem ipsum dolor sit amet, consectetaur adipisicing elit, sed do eiusmod tempor
incididunt ut labore et dolore magna aliqua. Lorem ipsum dolor sit amet, consectetaur
adipisicing elit, sed do eiusmod tempor incididunt ut labore et dolore magna aliqua.
</p>
</div>
```

3 After the closing `div` container, add the following line:

This ensures that all information appearing after the break will begin on a completely new line.

```
<br clear="all">
```

4 Create a new file, add the following code, and save it as `stagger.jss`:

Typically, you could hand code the stagger blocks in HTML. Because you are giving up precise control over your markup in favor of easy-use publishing, you need to think of a different way to achieve the effect.

```
if (placement == 0) {
     document.write('<span style="width:100px; display: inline;"></span>');
     placement++;
} else if (placement == 1) {
     document.write('<span style="width:100px; display: inline;"></span>');
     placement++;
} else if (placement == 2) {
     document.write('<span style="width:200px; display: inline;"></span>');
     placement++;
} else if (placement == 3) {
     document.write('<span style="width:150px; display: inline;"></span>');
     placement++;
} else if (placement == 4) {
     document.write('<span style="width:100px; display: inline;"></span>');
     placement++;
} else if (placement == 5) {
     document.write('<span style="width:150px; display: inline;"></span>');
     placement++;
}
```

DELVING DEEPER INTO SCRIPT

JavaScript can use "if" and "else if" statements, as it does in this chapter's example. As the script is called through the page, it runs a series of checks for the value of the `placement` variable. If the variable matches the expression in the parentheses, it executes the statement that follows. If it doesn't, it continues down the series:

```
if (expression) {
     statement
} else if (expression) {
     statement
     }
```

continues

106

Because you put the value of `placement` at 0 in the head of the document, the first time `stagger.js` runs, it will match the first expression:

```
if (placement == 0) {
document.write('<span style="width:100px; display:
➥inline;"></span>');
```

The double equal signs mean that you are testing a comparison between `placement` and 0. If they are equal, the expression is true and the script then proceeds to process the statement associated with it.

With this script, the JavaScript writes the code for a `span` tag, along with the inline style:

```
<span style="width:100px; display: inline;"></span>
```

Then the next step as the JavaScript runs its course is to increase the `placement`'s value by one through an operator. An operator allows for simple mathematics to be performed on variables:

```
placement++;
```

Essentially, what has happened through the first evoking of the `stagger.js` is that you have the JavaScript write a snippet of JavaScript and increase the value of `placement` from 0 to 1.

In the next steps, a similar process occurs. At each step, the value of `placement` increases by one, but also a different, predetermined HTML snippet is written, thus creating the stagger effect.

Table 6.1 Comparing Expressions to Actions

Comparison	What Happens
x == y	Returns true if x and y are equal.
x != y	Returns true if x and y are not equal.
x > y	Returns true if x is greater than y.
x < y	Returns true if x is less than y.
x >= y	Returns true if x is greater or equal to y.
x <= y	Returns true if x is less than or equal to y.
x && y	Returns true if x and y are true.
x || y	Returns true if x or y is true.
!x	Toggles the value of x.

COLLAPSING ENTRIES

Now that you have staggering text, it's time to create a list of items on your site that are larger than a paragraph or two. This could range from an essay or a focused rant that runs several pages or a section that is unrelated to your daily misadventures, but still defines who you are.

Tools, such as Blogger, give you the freedom to change the layout's template.

For example, say that you want people to read your recent entry before they dive into a list of side attractions. You don't want this list to be buried beneath the entries. Instead, you want to give readers an option to click on a collapsible list:

1   Add the following code to the script at the top of the HTML file:

In addition to the `placement` variable, you declared a variable called `features` to be 0 as well. The conditional performs similarly to the one in the `stagger.js` file, except it doesn't check to see if the variable is set to 0.

> **Note:** The `location.search` is the query portion of the URL that's currently being viewed in the web browser. In the following example of a URL, `location.search` is actually `?surprise=visible`.

2   Expand the `stagger.js` file and tweak the CSS to accommodate some extra block elements:

This sets up a comparison between two variables. If both equal true, the statement that follows will be executed. However, because you set the value features to 0 in the head of the HTML document, this expression fails and the script continues to read the next expression:

```
} else if ((placement == 1) &&
➥(features == 0)) {
```

Here, you see that placement needs to be 1 and variable features needs to be set to 0. As you have set your `stagger.js` file to be called several times throughout the page and increment `placement`'s value, it's conceivable that this expression might be returned as true and read the statement:

```
// item list collapsed
    document.writeln('<div class=
    "featuresgreen">');
```

Give readers an option to click on a collapsible entry. In this figure, it's closed.

```
<script type="text/javascript" language="JavaScript">
<!--
var placement = 0;
var features = 0;

        if (location.search.length > 0) {
                eval('var ' + location.search.substring(1));
                }
// -->
</script>
```

```
if (placement == 0) {
        document.write('<span style="width:100px; display:
        ➥inline;"></span>');
        placement++;
} else if ((placement == 1) && (features == 1)) {
// item list expanded
        document.writeln('<div class="featuresgreen">');
        document.writeln('collapse <a href="' +
document.location.pathname + '">
➥content listing &gt;</a></big><br> <br>');
        document.writeln('<div class="contentlisting">');
        document.writeln('site items go here');
        document.writeln('</div>');
        document.writeln('</div>');
// bumper
        document.write('<span style="width:100px; display:
        ➥inline;"></span>');
        placement++;
```

```
        document.writeln(' expand <a href="' + document.location.pathname
    ➥+'?features=1">content listing &gt;&gt;</a></big><br>');
        document.writeln('</div>');
// bumper
        document.write('<span style="width:100px; display:
    ➥inline;"></span>');
        placement++;

} else if (placement == 2) {
        document.write('<span style="width:200px; display:
    ➥inline;"></span>');
        placement++;
} else if (placement == 3) {
        document.write('<span style="width:150px; display:
    ➥inline;"></span>');
        placement++;
} else if (placement == 4) {
        document.write('<span style="width:100px; display:
    ➥inline;"></span>');
        placement++;
} else if (placement == 5) {
        document.write('<span style="width:150px; display:
    ➥inline;"></span>');
        placement++;
```

Along with the `bumper` and `placement` variable snippet, the JavaScript code
is asked to write some HTML. What this HTML code writes can be
understood in the following way:

Expand `<a href="currenturl.html?features=1">content listing</a>`

With the variable `features` now set to one, the full menu of items is visible
and nestled between the first journal entry and the second entry.

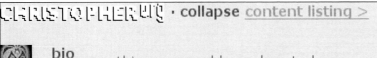

Opening the collapsible entry.

The final step? Mesh the JavaScript and template into a cohesive file.

3 Follow the steps outlined in the Blogger site's Publishing section to get your
blog working properly.

MORE MAGIC

Although Blogger is extremely popular, a couple of blog tools are worthy of a
note. Two of best known tools are the following:

- **Noah Grey's Greymatter (`http://noahgrey.com/greysoft/`)**—Similar in
  many aspects to Blogger except that Greymatter runs entirely on your own web
  server. The primary disadvantage is that you have to install the software on your
  own (or with the help of a programming friend). The advantage over Blogger is
  obvious: You run the engine on your setup without having to share the service
  with other users. If you do use this software, don't forget to buy Noah Grey
  something from his "wish list" as a form of payment for his hard work.

- **Manila (`http://manila.userland.com/`)**—Now a commercial product, Manila
  offers blogging as part of a complete web *Content Management System* (CMS).

With free tools and templates in place, personal-page enthusiasts can bypass the
nasty thought of opening up an FTP client or a bulky HTML editor. And if you
stop to think about that, it's really amazing. Instead of having to write up HTML
pages, connect to your ISP, upload files, create the proper link from to the content
from your main site, and so on, you simply use these tools to do the job for you.

Now that you have, at your disposal, a virtual printing press to tell the world
about everything that makes you special, you might want to think about how
you're going to present that information, and the kind of information you're willing to share with the world. A personal site should be personal, after all. But you
wouldn't leave your front door open in a high-crime area, would you? So here are
a few basic tips to ensure your safety when putting personal information on a blog:

- **Keep personal information, such as your home address and phone
  number, *off* your site**—Encourage people to use email to get in touch with
  you instead.

- **Some people are particularly protective of information that involves their children and loved ones**—Consider your feelings about this carefully—you might want to avoid putting pictures of children or any detailed information about your family online. Some people are less concerned; the risks are low, but then again, you don't know who is visiting your site. I encourage you to think about your own comfort levels of privacy.

- **Update your blog**—The point of having a blog is to keep your site fresh in a relatively painless way. If you're not going to update the blog, take it off your site.

Ultimately, the material you produce helps you connect with other people, inspire new ideas for your personal site, or might even help you launch a new business venture!

PART III

PROFESSIONAL

SITES

BUILDING A SITE WITH COMMUNITY FEEDBACK

"When your users put their words on

your site, it builds a powerful bond

between you and the user."

—DEREK M. POWAZEK

One of the great features of the Internet is its
ability to bring people together. A web site has
the potential to create a dialogue that breaches
borders and to establish a conversation that
unites people. In short, an excellent web site
builds a community.

Building a community for your web site requires
communication between you and your viewers.
Your site must always push information out. To
create a community, you need to provide a
forum that allows people to push information in.

Building a Site with Community Feedback

By John Kuhlman

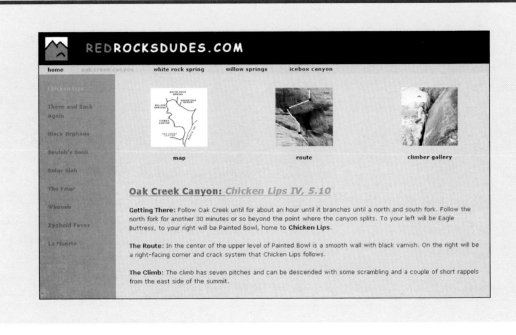

PROJECT SNAPSHOT

The problem: Designing an interface and building a site that supports viewer dialogue without creating an administrative nightmare for the person maintaining it.

This chapter is for anyone trying to build a basic, moderated community site for a group of people who share a common interest or pursuit.

TECHNICAL SPECS

The following are the technical specifications that you need:

- **Markup used**—XHTML 1.0
- *Document type definitions* **(DTDs) used**—Frameset and transitional

Here are the additional technologies or skills that you need to be familiar with:

- HTML
- *Cascading Style Sheets* (CSS)
- Frames
- Tables
- Forms
- A text editor, such as Notepad

Browser considerations: Design your site with flexibility in mind. Your audience might be viewing your site at 800 × 600 or at 1,024 × 768. Although the vast majority of your audience, as of this writing, uses Internet Explorer 5.*x* on Windows to view your web site, don't neglect the Navigator and Opera users. Each browser treats your HTML and your CSS differently.

Style sheets: You'll use a linked style sheet to format your content.

STRUCTURING THE SITE

The site will be composed of four separate frames containing the following:

- Header
- Main menu
- Sub menu
- Content

How the site's architecture looks: Remember that less is more. Your viewers have a goal when they come to visit your site. Your job is to help them find the information that they need, give them a forum to share their thoughts, and prevent them from getting lost in any clutter while they're there.

A well-planned community site can be compared to a good "hippie" commune. Your site provides the physical structure where people can congregate and share ideas. Your job is to create an environment where people can easily exchange those ideas.

Incorporating style sheets: CSS is used to control content and navigation. Using CSS with frames and tables prevents unnecessary coding and makes your site's appearance easier to modify down the road.

You're going to build a basic community site for rock climbers who pursue their craft in the famous Red Rocks, located a few miles from the glitzy Las Vegas Strip. What do they want from a web site dedicated to their community? Information on climbs and tips from other climbers about the routes that they use.

Going back to the analogy of a commune, think of yourself as the architect, designer, and general contractor. As the architect, you must design a site that's easy to use, where form follows function. No flashy stuff here, mister. As the designer, you need to make the site aesthetically pleasing, where your viewers are encouraged to communicate with each other. As the general contractor, you must build the structure and provide the tools that allows people to communicate—the strongest of human desires.

You will use XHTML to build a frameset that will compartmentalize navigation and content to allow for faster loading and easier maintenance when it comes time to expand the site's navigational capabilities. After you build the structure, spice it up with a little CSS. Then as the grand finale, you'll add a simple, but effective, doorway, so that viewers can share their thoughts.

GET ORGANIZED

Before you start building your site, you must do some prep work:

1 Copy the following graphics from this book's web site into a directory on your hard drive (called images):

- banner.jpg
- chicklips_route_t.jpg
- gallery_t.jpg
- oakcreek_t.jpg
- redrocksbox.jpg

2 Create a filler page called `blank.html`. Set a back-ground color of your choice, and put the phrase `Blank Page` in there.

You'll point to this page for areas of the site that you are not going to build in this chapter.

BUILDING THE FRAMESET

The first step of the project: Build the frameset. If you examine the completed site, you'll notice the four-part grid structure that you'll create. By drawing some horizontal lines across the grid, you'll have three rows (header, main menu, sub menu/content), with the third row being divided into two columns. You'll build the three rows first. The first row will contain the header page with the site name and logo. The second row will contain the main navigation menu. The third row will contain the sub-navigation menu and the content.

> **Note:** I placed the header and main menu areas in separate rows. This is because I want to have more control over each row. If I want to change the menu, I need only make the change to that file. If I want to update the header, I can easily do that by opening the file for the header.

1 Insert the following DTD in the first line of your text editor:

This XHTML frameset DTD must be used whenever you create a frameset document by using XHTML 1.0.

2 Save the file as `index.html`.

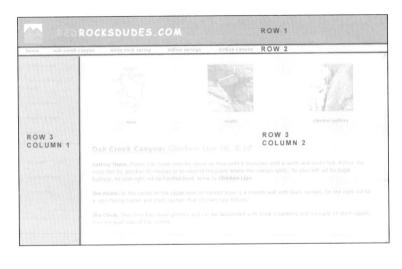

You can divide the site into a horizontal grid with three rows and two columns.

```
<!DOCTYPE html PUBLIC "-//W3C//DTD XHTML 1.0 Frameset//EN"
"http://www.w3.org/TR/xhtml1/DTD/xhtml1-frameset.dtd">
```

3 Add the following lines:

```
<html>
<head>
<title>Home of the Red Rocks Dudes</title>
</head>
<!-- WE'LL INSERT THE FRAME TAGS HERE -->

</html>
```

4 Create the frameset and define the height of the three rows:

The first row, or header, is set to 75 pixels high; the second row, or main menu, is set to 20 pixels high; the third row is set to *, or "take up the rest of the vertical space." Because the content length will vary, as will the viewers' browser sizes, you don't want to be boxed in by defining a height for this row.

```
<frameset rows="75,20,*" border="1" noresize frameborder="1"
➥framespacing="0">
<!-- INSERT FRAME SRC HERE -->
</frameset>
```

Caution: The `frameborder` and `framespacing` attributes are not available in the transitional DTD. However, to achieve cross-browser compatability and have no frame borders, you will have to employ this workaround. Your pages will not validate; however, they will work.

5 Before you use the `</frameset>` tag, define the first two rows by using the XHTML `<frame />` tag:

```
    <frame src="header.html" scrolling="no" name="header"
➥marginwidth="0" border="0" />
    <frame src="mainmenu.html" scrolling="no"
➥name="mainmenu.html" marginwidth="0" border="0" />
```

6 After the second `<frame />`, insert another frameset where you'd normally define the third row:

```
<frameset cols="170,*" border="1" noresize="noresize"
➥frameborder="1" framespacing="0">

</frameset>
```

Tip: Although the final site won't have visible frame borders, it's easier to troubleshoot your frames if you can see what they're framing by setting your border and frameborder width to 1.

This additional frameset is necessary because the third row is split into two columns.

7 Create a column for the sub menu and a column for the content within the third row:

You just created the structure for RedRocksDudes.com. Congratulations! Your complete code for `index.html` should look like Listing 7.1.

```
    <frame src="submenu.html" noresize="noresize" scrolling="auto"
➥name="submenu" marginwidth="0" border="0" />
    <frame src="chickenlips.html" scrolling="auto" name="content"
➥marginwidth="0" />
```

LISTING 7.1   COMPLETE CODE FOR INDEX.HTML

```
<!DOCTYPE HTML PUBLIC "-//W3C//DTD XHTML 1.0 Frameset//EN"
"http://www.w3.org/TR/xhtml1/DTD/xhtml1-frameset.dtd">

<html>
<head>
<title>Home of the Red Rocks Dudes</title>
</head>

<frameset rows="75,20,*" border="1" noresize="noresize" frameborder="1" framespacing="0">

        <frame src="header.html" scrolling="no" name="header" marginwidth="0" border="0" >

        <frame src="mainmenu.html" scrolling="no" name="mainmenu" marginwidth="0"
        border="0" >

        <frameset cols="170,*" border="1" noresize="noresize" frameborder="1"
        framespacing="0">

        <frame src="submenu.html" noresize="noresize" scrolling="auto" name="submenu"
        marginwidth="0" border="0" >

        <frame src="chickenlips.html" scrolling="auto" name="content" marginwidth="0" >

    </frameset>

</frameset>

</html>
```

BUILDING THE HEADER PAGE

Because each frame in the original schema requires a separate XHTML file to make it work, I'll lead you through the process of creating these files. Here, you create a new document called `header.html`:

1 Add the DTD and set the page's background color to black (#000000):

I'm using a transitional XHTML DTD for the internal pages. The frameset DTD is *only* used for framesets. This is the only way to create valid XHTML 1.0 frames. The frameset must have the specialized XHTML 1.0 frameset DTD declaration, whereas the internal pages must have a `DOCTYPE` of transitional or strict because those pages are *not* framesets. Rather, they are individual HTML or XHTML pages.

```
<!DOCTYPE html PUBLIC "-//W3C//DTD XHTML 1.0 Transitional//EN"
"DTD/xhtml1-transitional.dtd">

<html>
<head>
<title></title>
</head>

<body bgcolor="#000000">

</body>
</html>
```

2 Before the </body> tag, add the following lines:

This code creates a table with one row and two cells to house the logo (`redrocksbox.jpg`) and banner (`banner.jpg`).

```
<table border="0" cellpadding="15" cellspacing="0">
<tr>

  <td><img src="images/redrocksbox.jpg" width="50" height="50" border="0"
➥alt="" /></td>

  <td><img src="images/banner.jpg" width="375" height="35" border="0"
➥alt="RedRocksDudes.com" /></td>

</tr>
</table>
```

3 Call up `index.html` to look at your progress.

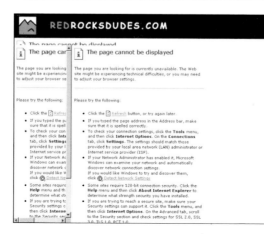

View the header frame that was added in step 2. At this point, you can see the beginnings of your site. The pages that can't be displayed are the additional pages that you need to complete.

Adding the Menu

The next phase of this project is to create a file called `mainmenu.html`. This page will be home to the main, or top-tier, navigation menu. To add the menu, follow these steps:

1 Add the DTD and set a gray background:

```
<!DOCTYPE html PUBLIC "-//W3C//DTD XHTML 1.0 Transitional//EN"
"DTD/xhtml1-transitional.dtd">

<html>
<head>
<title></title>
</head>

<body bgcolor="#cccccc">

</body>
</html>
```

2 Prior to the `</body>` tag, set up a table with one row and five cells:

This table controls the positioning of the main menu. Notice that, within the `<a>` tags, the markup tells the browser to load each page in the content frame.

```
<table border="0" cellpadding="0" cellspacing="0">
<tr>
  <td width="75"><p><a href="blank.html" target="content">home</a></p></td>
  <td width="160"><p><a href="oakcreek.html" target="content">oak creek canyon</a></p></td>
  <td width="160"><p><a href="blank.html" target="content">white rock spring</a></p></td>
  <td width="140"><p><a href="blank.html" target="content">willow springs</a></p></td>
  <td width="150"><p><a href="blank.html" target="content">icebox canyon</a></p></td>
</tr>
</table>
```

Tip: Because you're using text for navigation, you'll have to tinker with the table width for each cell. Just eyeball it so an even space exists between each cell. Why not just use `cellpadding` or `cellspacing` to control the space? Because the main menu frame is only 20 pixels high, you don't have much room to play with, and `cellpadding` and `cellspacing` add space to all four sides of the cell. Go ahead and set your `cellpadding` to 10 and see what happens. Another more contemporary alternative is to use style sheet layouts. You can accomplish this with relative ease, but many browsers don't support it. See the section, "More Magic" at the end of this chapter for the technique.

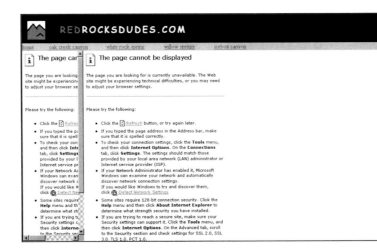

Set up the navigation using a table. The target to content means that all the markup will load in the lower-right portion of the frame structure.

BUILDING THE SUB MENU

So far, you built the header and main navigation. In this exercise, you create the sub menu:

1 Declare the DOCTYPE and set the background color:

This time, the background color is reflective of the Red Rocks.

```
<!DOCTYPE html PUBLIC "-//W3C//DTD XHTML 1.0 Transitional//EN"
"DTD/xhtml1-transitional.dtd">

<html>
<head>
<title></title>
<link rel="stylesheet" type="text/css" href="redrocksstyle.css" />
</head>

<body bgcolor="#cc6600">

</body>
</html>
```

2 Add the following code to submenu.html:

This action sets the base target so all the links that you'll be adding will automatically load to the content page.

```
<base target="content" />
</head>
```

3 Add the links, as follows:

These lines add the sub menu choices. You could use a table again to align the sub menu navigation items, but there's really no need to because it's just a series of one-line paragraphs. Remember to keep it simple.

```
<p><a href="chickenlips.html">Chicken Lips</a></p>
<p><a href="blank.html">There and Back Again</a></p>
<p><a href="blank.html">Black Orpheus</a></p>
<p><a href="blank.html">Beulah's Book</a></p>
<p><a href="blank.html">Solar Slab</a></p>
<p><a href="blank.html">The Friar</a></p>
<p><a href="blank.html">Whoosh</a></p>
<p><a href="blank.html">Xyphoid Fever</a></p>
<p><a href="blank.html">La Muerte</a></p>


</body>
</html>
```

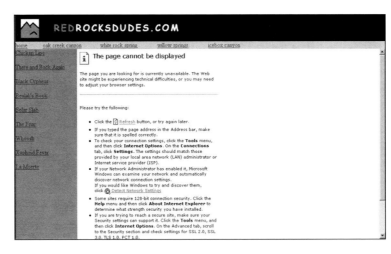

Compare your work to the sub menu navigation you just built.

CREATING THE MAIN CONTENT PAGE

You're finally ready to add the main content, which includes the following:

- A thumbnail map to Oak Creek Canyon that can be enlarged when it's clicked

- A thumbnail route diagram of Chickenlips that can be enlarged when it's clicked

- A thumbnail image of photographs supplied by viewers of climbers on Chickenlips

- A text description on how to get to Oak Creek Canyon ("Getting There")

- A text description on how to find Chickenlips ("The Route")

- A text description of the climb ("The Climb")

- A moderated forum for climbers to share their thoughts about Chickenlips

Again, you use a table to format the main content page:

1 Add the standard opener and set the background color to a semi-sandstone:

```
<!DOCTYPE html PUBLIC "-//W3C//DTD XHTML 1.0 Transitional//EN"
"DTD/xhtml1-transitional.dtd">


<html>
<head>
<title>redrocksdudes.com</title>
```

continues

124

continued

```
</head>

<body bgcolor="#ffcc66">

</body>
</html>
```

2 Prior to the </body> tag, use a table to set up a three-column, two-row layout for content (refer to Listing 7.1). Begin with the table attributes:

```
<table border="0" cellpadding="20" cellspacing="10">
```

3 Add the first row:

This sets up the images for the Map, Route, and Climber galleries.

```
<!-- ROW 1 -->
<tr>
    <td align="center"><a href="blank.html"><img src="images/oakcreek_t.jpg"
➥width="125" height="125" border="0" alt="map" />
    <span class="caption">map</span></a></td>
    <td align="center"><a href="blank.html"><img
➥src="images/chicklips_route_t.jpg" width="125" height="125" border="0"
➥alt="Chicken Lips" />
    <span class="caption">route</span></a></td>
    <td align="center"><a href="blank.html"><img src="images/gallery_t.jpg"
➥width="125" height="125" border="0" alt="Climber's Gallery" />
    <span class="caption">climber gallery</span></a></td>
</tr>
```

4 Add the second row below the first row and wrap up the table, as follows:

```
<!-- ROW 2 -->
<tr>
    <td colspan="3">
    <h3>Oak Creek Canyon: <em>Chicken Lips IV, 5.10</em></h3>
    <p><b>Getting There:</b> Follow Oak Creek until for about an hour until it branches
until a north and south fork. Follow the north fork for another 30 minutes or so beyond
the point where the canyon splits. To your left will be Eagle Buttress, to your right
will be Painted Bowl, home to <b>Chicken Lips</b>.</p>

    <p><b>The Route:</b> In the center of the upper level of Painted Bowl is a smooth
wall with black varnish. On the right will be a right-facing corner and crack system
that Chicken Lips follows.</p>
```

You now have the structure for your content pages in place. Next, you'll give the climbers a way to submit their comments to the site and add some CSS to turn this clunker of a site into something more aesthetically pleasing.

continued

```
    <p><b>The Climb:</b> The climb has seven pitches and can be
descended with some scrambling and a couple of short rappels
from the east side of the summit.</p>
    </td>
  </tr>
</table>
```

Note: Web designers either love or hate frames. Frames can be a wonderful friend for your viewers, saving them from reloading entire pages each time they move to another section in your site. Frames can also be your worst enemy if a viewer gets hold of a page, such as `chickenlips.html`, outside of the safety of the frame structure. At that point, all navigation is lost and your viewer's stranded in cyberspace. An antiquated, but still useful workaround to prevent your frame pages from being loaded without the frame involves simply inserting the following JavaScript in the `<head>` section of each page (except in the master frameset page, such as `index.html`):

```
<script language="JavaScript">
<!-- Hide from older browsers
if (window == top) top.location.href =
"index.html";
// -->
</script>
```

This code was originally used to direct older browsers that weren't capable of utilizing frames to another non-frames section of the web site. In this case, you can use it to redirect everyone to your home page.

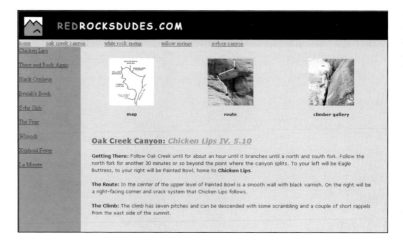

Create the general structure for content areas, allowing for a pleasant visual esthetic and combined opportunity to add technology.

ADDING A VIEWER COMMENT SECTION

What's a community site without a way for your viewers to exchange ideas? In this section, you'll add a simple, but safe, method for your viewers to submit comments to the site. Rather than tie into a database like MySQL and get into some PHP, which you do in the next chapter, here you'll create a simple email link. Although this method doesn't allow for instantaneous posting to the site, it is easy to set up and it also prevents people from posting profanity or off-topic comments.

1 Create a third and fourth row for the table in `chickenlips.html`:

The third row holds an email link, and you will put the comments from the climbers in the fourth row. Adding the `?SUBJECT=CHICKENLIPS` to your `<a href mailto>` tag inserts `CHICKENLIPS` into the subject line of email messages. This trick helps you sort what will hopefully be a flood of email comments to the site. As each comment arrives in your inbox, simply add it as the next paragraph in the table cell. It's not pretty, but you're basically in business with a forum on your site.

```
<!-- ROW 3 -->
<tr>
    <td colspan="3">
    <hr />
    <p><a href="mailto:dude@redrocksdude.com?SUBJECT=CHICKENLIPS">Share your thoughts
on Chickenlips</a></p>
    <hr />
    </td>
</tr>


<!-- ROW 4 -->
<tr>
    <td colspan="3">
    <p><b>03.11.01 - Mike T:</b> Watch for a bad bolt on Pitch 4, just after
the traverse.</p>
    <p><b>02.28.01 - Jan S:</b> Dudes, I left my favorite t-shirt up near
the crack after the 5th pitch, I'll give $5 to anyone who brings it back. Call
Jan at 555-5555.</p></td>
</tr>
</table>
```

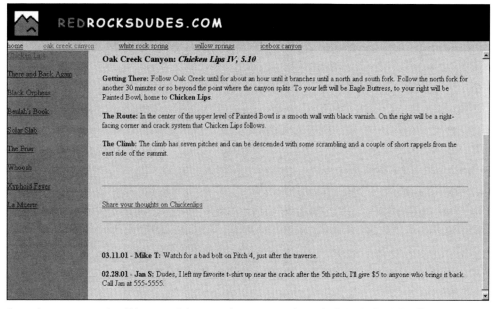

Create the comment section. This approach is a manual one a more advanced solution is detailed in Chapter 8, "Creating a Complex Community Site."

CREATING THE EXTERNAL STYLE SHEET

Keep your text editor open, because next you'll create the external style sheet that will control the look of the entire site. Before you define any of your styles, go back to mainmenu.html, submenu.html, and chickenlips.html to create a link to the currently empty style sheet (redrocksstyle.css).

1   Add the following line to each page (if it's not already there):

Your pages are now linked to the style sheet.

```
<head>

<link rel="stylesheet" type="text/css" href="redrocksstyle.css" />
</head>
```

2   Open redrocksstyle.css and define what the links will look like globally:

Here, you're adding some color to the main menu navigation.

```
a {
        text-decoration: none;
}

a:link   {
        color:   #336600;
        font-weight: bold;
}

a:visited {
        color:   #cc9900;
        font-weight: bold;
}

a:active {
        color:   #cccc00;
        font-weight: bold;
}

a:hover {
        color:   #ff0000;
        text-decoration: underline;
        font-weight: bold;
}
```

3 Create a separate class for the main menu navigation text:

Creating a new class enables you to make the main menu navigation text look different from the rest.

```
p.main {
        font-size: 8pt;
        margin-left: 20px;
        margin-top: 0px;
        font-family: verdana,sans-serif;
        font-weight:bold;
}
```

4 Define an ID for the navigation text:

By giving the navigation text a unique ID, you prevent if from being affected by the main A: style that you previously defined.

```
#navbar a:link {
    color: #000000;
}

#navbar a:hover {
    color: #ff0000;
}
```

Note: In Chapter 1, "About Web Markup: XML, HTML, XHTML," the concept of classes was introduced. An ID is a specialty class in CSS. It's preceded by a hash (pound) sign (#) and the name of the class. Classes of this type ensure that the style you create won't be affected by any other defined style.

5 Open `mainmenu.html` and add the `class="main"` `id="navbar"` to each of the `<p>` tags:

This sets up the `class` attribute to relate to the properties defined by `.main` in the style sheet, and identifying, through the `id` attribute and the `#navbar` class, that these particular links are part of that class.

```
<tr>
        <td width="75"><p class="main" id="navbar"><a href="blank.html"
➥target="content">home</a></p></td>
        <td width="160"><p class="main" id="navbar"><a href="chickenlips.html"
➥target="content">oak creek canyon</a></p></td>
        <td width="160"><p class="main" id="navbar"><a href="blank.html"
➥target="content">white rock spring</a></p></td>
        <td width="140"><p class="main" id="navbar"><a href="blank.html"
➥target="content">willow springs</a></p></td>
        <td width="150"><p class="main" id="navbar"><a href="blank.html"
➥target="content">icebox canyon</a></p></td>
</tr>
```

6 Create a class to position the sub menu `<p>` tags by adding the following to `redrocksstyle.css`:

```
p.sub {
        font-size: 8pt;
        margin-left: 20px;
        margin-top: 20px;
        font-family: verdana,sans-serif;
}
```

7 Open `submenu.html` and change all your `<p>` tags to

All your paragraphs now take on the property values described in the `.sub` class.

```
<p class="sub">
```

8 In `redrocksstyle.css`, create a style for the map, route map, and gallery captions by adding the following:

```
p.caption {
        font-size:8pt;
        text-align:center;
        font-family:verdana;sans-serif;
        margin:0px;
}
```

9 Open `chickenlips.html` and change the `<p>` tags to

```
<tr>
    <td align="center"><a href="blank.html"><img
➥src="images/oakcreek_t.jpg" width="125" height="125" border="0"
➥alt="map">
    <p class="caption">map</p></a></td>
    <td align="center"><a href="blank.html"><img
➥src="images/chicklips_route_t.jpg" width="125" height="125"
➥border="0" alt="Chicken Lips">
    <p class="caption">route</p></a></td>
    <td align="center"><a href="blank.html"><img src="images/
➥gallery_t.jpg" width="125" height="125" border="0"
➥alt="Climber's Gallery">
    <p class="caption">climber gallery</p></a></td>
</tr>
```

10 Next, set up page styles for "Oak Creek Canyon: Chicken Lips IV, 5.10":

Because you want to make the route name italic and a lighter shade of green, you assign an <em> to that section and define a style for <em> in `redrocksstyle.css`.

```css
h3 {
        color: #336600;
        font-size: 14pt;
        font-family: verdana,sans-serif;
        font-weight: bold;
        text-decoration: underline;
}

em {
        color:#669900;
}
```

11 Define a style for the standard <p> tag in `redrocksstyle.css`:

```css
p {
        color: black;
        margin-top: 10px;
        margin-left: 0px;
        margin-right: 0px;
        font-size: 10pt;
        line-height: 14pt;
        font-family: verdana,sans-serif;
}
```

12 Create a unique look for climber comments in `redrocksstyle.css`:

You want the climbers' comments to stand out a bit from the official content, so they need their own look.

```css
p.comment {
        font-size:10pt;
        line-height:14pt;
        font-family:courier,serif;
}
```

13 Close `redrocksstyle.css` and edit the <p> tags for the comments section in `chickenlips.html`:

At this point, you are the proud owner of a stylin' basic community web site. Congratulations! In the next chapter, you build this site to enable climbers to post their own messages directly.

```html
<p class="comment">
```

More Magic

Naturally, several approaches exist to building a community site. The following are just a few options that you have to play with:

- Go crazy with CSS. Change the font colors, link attributes, and so on.
- Experiment with various frame rows and column sizes.
- If you're a graphics wizard and know basic JavaScript, replace all the navigational text with buttons and mouse-over effects.

The more you experiment, the more you'll find clever ways of using style, frame structures, and interactive elements.

Alternatives to Table Layout

It is undeniable that a shift away from tables toward the power of style sheets is a strong one. However, as you are by now well aware, support for style sheets or aspects of style sheets might not be available to many of your site visitors. As such, many designers still opt to design with tables.

Using the `div` element or absolute positioning can be helpful in creating familiar table layouts. A great tutorial on using a range of these techniques can be found at `http://glish.com/css/`.

Designing Community Sites

In preparation for Chapter 8, which takes the work you did here and builds an interactive forum into the site, you'll need to organize a bit.

So, grab a cocktail napkin and start listing the types of conversations that your viewers might want on your site. Better yet, observe how members of a club or group interact with one another. What do they talk about? Do they complain about products? Do they offer advice to one another? Do they communicate with similar groups? Do cliques exist within the main group? Find common topics of interest and use them to help create the interactive portion of your site.

CREATING A COMPLEX COMMUNITY SITE

"Digital worlds form a web of community. They connect

people from across the planet to form virtual communities.

They dissolve the barriers of time and location, and in

their place create ties of interest and, perhaps, even a

new form of global consciousness."

—STEVEN HOLTZMAN, *DIGITAL MOSAICS*

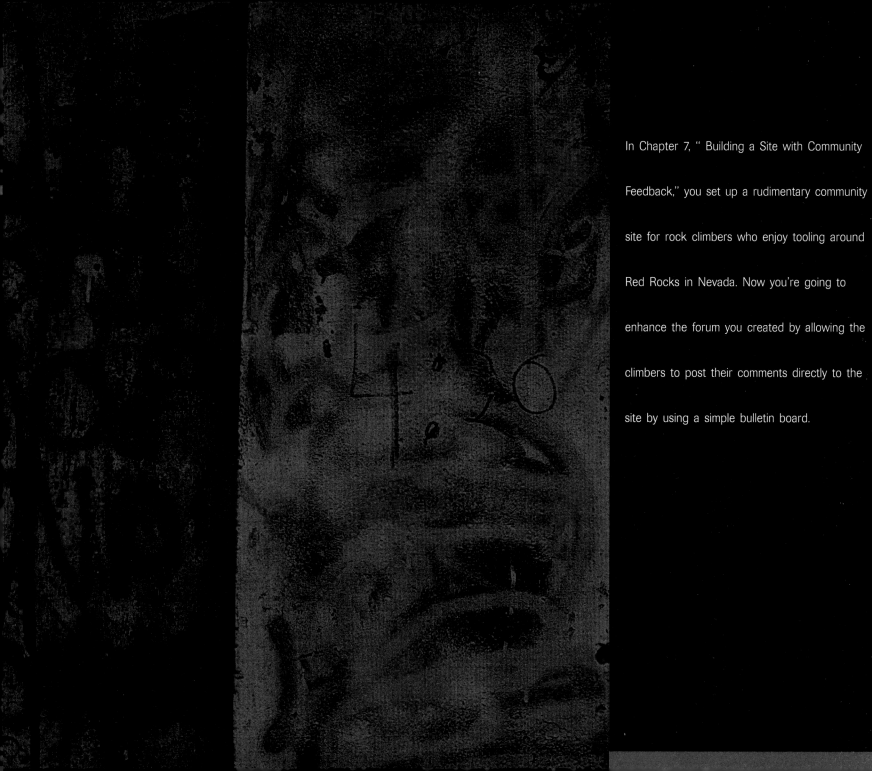

In Chapter 7, " Building a Site with Community Feedback," you set up a rudimentary community site for rock climbers who enjoy tooling around Red Rocks in Nevada. Now you're going to enhance the forum you created by allowing the climbers to post their comments directly to the site by using a simple bulletin board.

Creating a Complex Community Site

By John Kuhlman

PROJECT SNAPSHOT

The problem: Creating a forum where viewers can easily add content to a site and start a dialogue with other people without using complex backend databases.

This chapter is for anyone who's trying to enhance the features of a community site and who has a basic familiarity with PHP.

TECHNICAL SPECS

The following are the technical specifications that you need:

- **Markup used**—XHTML 1.0
- *Document type definition* (**DTD**) **used**—Frameset, transitional

Most of the work that you'll do in this chapter is focused on using PHP to create a user forum. One of the big challenges for webmasters is trying to find suitable methods to achieve integrated results, including a great front end and working technology. After all, markup doesn't exist in a vacuum. You can write HTML and *Cascading Style Sheets* (CSS) 'til the cows come home, but without the ability to add function and interactivity to a site, that site will remain limited. In this chapter, you get a chance to stretch and explore techniques that go beyond markup, but work with markup to make your site come to life.

Here are the additional technologies or skills you need to be familiar with:

- HTML
- CSS
- Frames
- Tables
- Forms
- PHP
- A text editor, such as Notepad

Browser considerations: Design your site with flexibility in mind. Your audience might view your site at 800×600 or at $1,024 \times 768$. Although the vast majority of your audience, as of this writing, uses Internet Explorer 5.*x* on Windows to view your site, don't neglect the Navigator and Opera users. Each browser treats your HTML and CSS differently.

Style sheets: Because you'll be using frames in this chapter, you'll use linked style sheets to format your content.

STRUCTURING THE SITE

The site will be composed of four separate frames contained within `index.html`:

- Header
- Main menu
- Sub menu
- Content

You build upon the site that was created in Chapter 7.

How the site's architecture looks: In keeping with the theme of simplicity, you want to keep your viewers from unnecessary page-hopping. The bulletin board feature will be added to the bottom of the existing Chicken Lips page.

Incorporating style sheets: CSS will be used to control content and navigation. Because HTML and XHTML tags can be embedded in PHP, you utilize the power of CSS to format your bulletin board entries.

HOW IT WORKS

In the first community project (refer to Chapter 7), you built a site that created a simple dialogue with its viewers. Visitors clicked a link that allowed them to submit their comments about the route Chicken Lips through email. The person maintaining the site read the email, determined if it fit the topic, and added it to the site with standard HTML.

At this point, assume that you expanded the site to provide coverage on most of the routes at Red Rocks. In addition to Chicken Lips, that means you're providing content and accepting email comments on approximately 250 other routes.

To save your sanity, it's time to automate the process with a little PHP and let your climbers bypass you and post their comments directly to each route page.

What's PHP? It's a set of server-side scripting tools that was known as *Personal Home Page Tools* when it was originally developed in 1994. In the spirit of Open Source Software Development, folks from around the world contributed to its growth and power. According to the PHP manual, "The goal of the language is to allow web developers to write dynamically generated pages quickly." A great resource for more PHP information is `www.php.net`.

In a nutshell, PHP can gather data from forms, access databases, and generate content on the fly. Plus, it has several other powerful features. For this project, you're going to insert some PHP to capture information that the climbers submit through a form, and write that information back on the same page.

INSTALLING APACHE

Apache is a freeware web server that typically runs on Unix-type servers, but also runs on Windows 95/98/NT. You need to make your computer think that it's a web server in order to parse the PHP. First, you need to install Apache:

1 Download the latest version of the Windows binary file (`*.exe` extension) from `http://www.apache.org/`, and double-click the icon to install the software

2 Keep the defaults for the Apache installation directory and the name that will appear on the Start menu, and choose Typical for Installation Type.

The default directory is `C:\Program Files\Apache Group\Apache\` and the default name is Apache Web Server.

3 Copy all the files and images from the project you built in Chapter 7 into the `htdocs` directory.

In addition to other system directories, the installation program creates a default document root called `htdocs`, just below `C:\Program Files\Apache Group\Apache\`. This area is generally used for documents and some scripts.

4 Choose Start, Programs, Apache Web Server, Start Apache. If you're running Windows NT, select Install Apache as a Service.

To stop Apache, simply select Stop Apache.

5 Open your browser and type `http://127.0.0.1`. This is an IP address that points to your local PC (also referred to as localhost).

You should now see the Welcome to Apache! Page.

> **Note:** If you don't see the Welcome page, or if you're having other difficulties, consult the Apache documentation or the Apache FAQ for guidance at `apache.org`.

Use the Apache Installation wizard to install Apache Web Server.

Get Apache up and running.

INSTALLING PHP

The hard part is over. Installing PHP is about as simple as it gets:

1 Download the latest Windows PHP executable file from the Downloads section of `www.php.net`.

2 Extract the file that you downloaded to a directory, such as `C:\PHP\`.

3 Change the value of `extension_dir` to point to `C:\PHP\`.

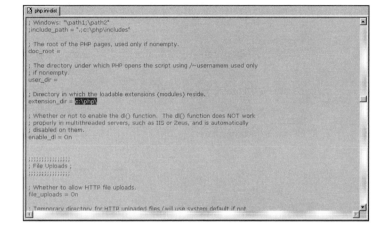

Change the value of the directory.

```
; Windows: "\path1;\path2"
;include_path = ".;c:\php\includes"

; The root of the PHP pages, used only if nonempty.
doc_root =

; The directory under which PHP opens the script using /~usernamem used only
; if nonempty.
user_dir =

; Directory in which the loadable extensions (modules) reside.
extension_dir = c:\php\

; Whether or not to enable the dl() function.  The dl() function does NOT work
; properly in multithreaded servers, such as IIS or Zeus, and is automatically
; disabled on them.
enable_dl = On


;;;;;;;;;;;;;;;;
; File Uploads ;
;;;;;;;;;;;;;;;;

; Whether to allow HTTP file uploads.
file_uploads = On

; Temporary directory for HTTP unloaded files (will use system default if not
```

4 Change the value of `doc_root` to point to the document root of your Apache Web Server `C:\Program Files\Apache Group\Apache\htdocs\`.

Change the value of the document root.

```
; Windows: "\path1;\path2"
;include_path = ".;c:\php\includes"

; The root of the PHP pages, used only if nonempty.
doc_root = c:\Program Files\Apache Group\Apache\htdocs\

; The directory under which PHP opens the script using /~usernamem used only
; if nonempty.
user_dir =

; Directory in which the loadable extensions (modules) reside.
extension_dir = c:\php\

; Whether or not to enable the dl() function.  The dl() function does NOT work
; properly in multithreaded servers, such as IIS or Zeus, and is automatically
; disabled on them.
enable_dl = On


;;;;;;;;;;;;;;;;
; File Uploads ;
;;;;;;;;;;;;;;;;

; Whether to allow HTTP file uploads.
file_uploads = On

; Temporary directory for HTTP unloaded files (will use system default if not
```

CONFIGURE AND TEST APACHE/PHP

Now that you have Apache and PHP installed, they need to be configured so they can play with each other. In essence, you tell Apache what to do when it encounters a file that ends with .php3, .phtml, or .php. To do this, you need to edit the httpd.conf file.

1 Add the following lines to the httpd.conf found in the C:\ProgramFiles\Apache Group\conf\ directory:

These lines tell Apache to parse the PHP code by running the php.exe program. In the next steps, you see if you were successful by testing the configuration.

```
ScriptAlias /php/ "c:/php/"
AddType application/x-httpd-php .php3 .phtml .php
Action application/x-httpd-php "/php/php.exe"
```

2 Start your Apache Web Server, or restart it if it's currently running. Create a text file called test.php and type the following:

```
<?php echo "Hello Ma! I'm using PHP!";?>
```

3 Save the file in C:\Program Files\Apache Group\ htdocs\.

4 Open your browser to http://127.0.0.1/test.php.

In your browser window, you should see the following line:

Hello Ma! I'm using PHP!

Note: If you don't see the message or run into difficulties, read the PHP FAQ at http://www.php.net.

Tip: If the installation and configuration details make you squeamish, you might want to consider trying a third-party freeware program that automatically installs and configures PHP and Apache to your desktop. Go to http://www.php.net for details, or visit this book's web site (www.xhtml-resources.com/magic/) for a complete list of resources.

Get PHP ready to go.

CREATE THE COMMENT FORM

Now that you have the administrative details out of the way, it's time to add some interactivity to RedRocksDudes.com. The first step is to create the submission form:

1 Open `chickenlips.html` and find the third row, which looks like this:

```
<tr>
    <td colspan="3">
    <hr />
    <p><a>
href="mailto:dude@redrocksdude.com?SUBJECT=
CHICKENLIPS">Share your thoughts on Chicken
Lips</a></p>
    <hr />
    </td>

</tr>
```

2 Replace the `<a>` tag with the form:

Notice that you're creating a three-part form: an input section for the climber's name; a message area where the climber can share some fairly extensive wisdom; and a Submit button that will pass all the information to your PHP script for processing.

```
<h3>Graffiti: <em>Chicken Lips</em></h3>
    <p>Use our handy-dandy form below to share any thoughts or tips about Chicken
Lips.</p>
    <form method="post">
    <p><b>Name:</b> <input name="name" type="text" size="25"></p>
    <p><b>Your Wisdom:</b><br /> <textarea name="wisdom" rows="5" cols="45">
</textarea></p>
    <input name="submit" type="submit" value="enlighten us!" />
    </form>
```

3 In the fourth row of your table, replace the sample feedback with some PHP:

```php
<?php

    if ($wisdom)
        {
        $name = strip_tags($name);
        $wisdom = strip_tags($wisdom,"<a>,<b>,<i>,<p>,<br>");
        if (get_magic_quotes_gpc())
            {
            $wisdom = stripslashes($wisdom);
            $name = stripslashes($name);
            }
        $wisdom = ereg_replace("\r\n\r\n", "\n<p>", $wisdom);
```

Because this book isn't about PHP, I'm not going to explain the code line by line. To combine PHP with HTML/XHTML, the PHP code must be set apart, or escaped, from the HTML/XHTML. This is achieved by the following:

```
<?php
// PHP code goes here.
?>
```

The PHP inserted into the table essentially processes the form input, strips some HTML tags from the climber's comments so they cannot run any JavaScript or other nasty executable files, and writes it to a new file, called chickenlips.txt. chickenlips.txt is then reinserted back into chickenlips.php on the fly.

4 Save the file as chickenlips.php.

Now type a name and comment in the form, click the Submit button, and presto! You see your information posted at the bottom of the page.

Tip: Make sure that you don't forget to change all your anchor tag references from chickenlips.html to chickenlips.php.

continued

```
        $date = date("l, F j Y, h:i a");
        $wisdom = "<b>$name </b> – $date<br /> $wisdom <br /><hr />\n";
        $fp = fopen (basename($PHP_SELF, '.php') . ".txt", "a");
        fwrite ($fp, $wisdom );
        fclose ($fp);
        }


    @readfile(basename(($PHP_SELF . ."/.php")));
?>
```

Test the file in a browser. You can see the simple form input area and an example of the posted results.

Add CSS to the Visitor's Comments

The beauty of PHP is that you can format the text that the form spits out. All you need to do is insert the following tag (previously defined in the last step) in the PHP, as follows:

```
$wisdom = "<p class=comment><b>$name </b> --
➥$date<br /> $words <br /><hr />\n";
```

Congratulations! You just created a fully functioning bulletin board.

More Magic

Managing a community is like hosting a neighborhood block party. You must throw a shindig of epic proportions to attract the neighbors, provide an eclectic menu of food and beverages, entertain the masses so they will want to come to your next party; all the while, keeping the Clampetts from the next cul de sac from hanging around. In essence, you have to be discriminatingly inclusive. The following are some general guidelines that you might want to consider:

- **Post rules**—Every party has its set of written and unwritten rules. Provide participation guidelines so there's no confusion on what behavior will be tolerated and not tolerated.

- **Encourage repeat visits**—Viewer turnover can be a problem. People will often visit your site to see what goodies you have to offer. If you don't keep their interest, they won't come back. Keep your material fresh and timely.

- **Identify leaders**—Every community site has a group of visitors who enjoy your site as "regulars." If they make worthwhile contributions, cultivate their talent. Offer them a byline to write short features or product reviews for you (or some other form of compensation).

- **Take care of the new people**—Every site that has a guestbook or bulletin board has a question that never gets answered. Although you might not know the answer, respond to the viewer and at least acknowledge his or her presence. Everyone likes to be loved—at least a little.

- **Keep it clean**—There's always an obnoxious viewer who uses your site as a forum to anonymously trash someone. Delete his or her comments to keep peace in the family and to keep everyone on topic.

  Because your site visitors can submit posts and carry on dialogues with each other without your participation, there's a risk that some folks might start using your forum to say nasty things about you, each other, or life in general.

To remove these rude comments, simply open the chickenlips.txt file and erase the undesirable entries.

Your community site, just like a neighborhood party, eventually takes on a life of its own. Let it. Stay close by to give it a guiding hand from time to time, but allow your viewers to take it where they want. Your job is to make sure that they have the environment where they can share information and enjoy each other's company.

As PHP continues to grow in popularity, smart people are constantly coming up with nifty new uses for this simple and powerful little language. If your interest has been piqued by PHP, here are a few other areas where you can use this gem on your site:

- Set up a shopping-cart system.

- Run online surveys.

- Manage your banner ad program.

- Manage an email subscriber and mailing list.

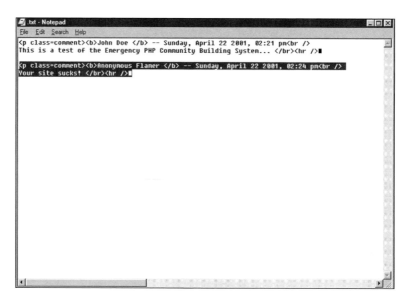

To fix an undesired entry, open the text file and delete the entry.

- Manage your site's content.

- Run a classified advertising section.

- Manipulate images.

- Analyze your web traffic.

- Establish user authentication.

- Manage site navigations.

- Run online auctions.

There's no shortage of what you can do with PHP and a little creativity. For example, one PHP-focused web site has more than 1,700 sample PHP scripts covering 72 topics. After you understand the basics, you can essentially manage nearly every function of your site with PHP.

SETTING UP A STOREFRONT

"Once the losers leave the dot-com arena,

the real games can commence."

—LARRY DIGNAN, *ZIFF-DAVIS REPORTER*

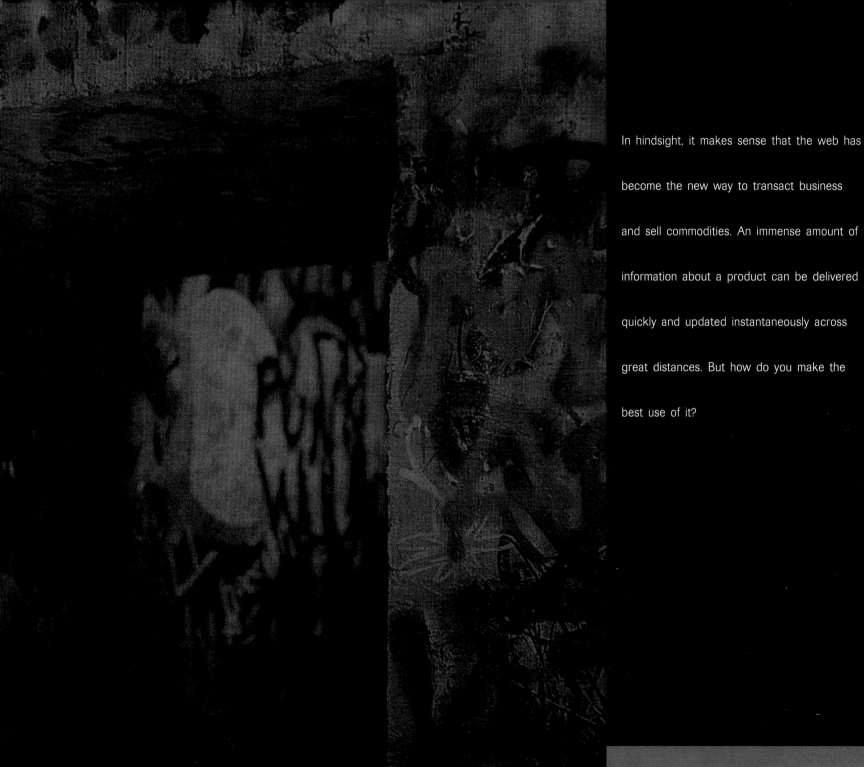

In hindsight, it makes sense that the web has become the new way to transact business and sell commodities. An immense amount of information about a product can be delivered quickly and updated instantaneously across great distances. But how do you make the best use of it?

Project 8

Setting Up a Storefront

By Jason Cranford Teague

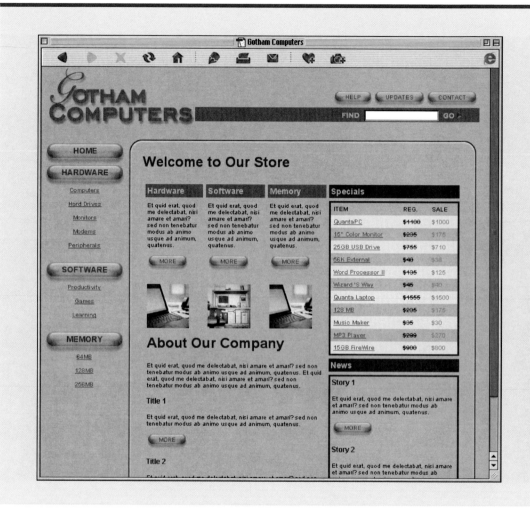

In this project, Gotham Computers sells computer software, hardware, and memory chips online. Visitors can search or browse through the online catalog to fulfil their computer needs. Using the Gotham Computers example, you look at the best practices for setting up a storefront and explore techniques for using *Cascading Style Sheets* (CSS) to create graphic buttons, format content from a database, tailor the CSS (depending on the browser), and other useful techniques for creating a compelling layout.

PROJECT SNAPSHOT

The problem: You can't sell everything on the web, especially items that the customers might want to touch and feel before giving up their hard-earned cash. Ironically, however, computers are a great way to sell computers and computer peripherals. Therefore, it makes a great example for conveying some important development issues when it comes to a commerce-based site.

This chapter is for anyone looking to create an online store.

TECHNICAL SPECS

The following are the technical specifications that you need to set up a storefront:

- **Markup used**—HTML 4.01

- *Document type definition* **(DTD) used**—Transitional

Although you can also use XHTML 1.0 transitional for this exercise, HTML 4.01 was chosen because it's probably more familiar to readers. This chapter asks you to successfully bridge a combination of approaches for presentation and, as such, is an excellent example of transitional design. As you work through the project, you'll find complex tables and spliced graphics help create part of the visual effect—CSS takes up the slack and adds special effects. However, translating this code into XHTML would not be difficult. If you want to learn more about translating HTML into XHTML, check out my article about this topic at www.webbedenvironments.com/v02/02_27.html.

This approach is becoming more common as web authors move away from poorly formed HTML to a more sophisticated separation of document and presentation. Balancing presentation successfully with markup and CSS is an especially good approach for audiences—such as those people who are buying computer components online—that are largely more sophisticated. Typically, this audience will have up-to-date browsers. But, this approach does provide some backward support so as to not completely close the store to those people without the most-advanced technologies.

Here are the additional technologies or skills you need:

- Familiarity with HTML

- Familiarity with web graphic production

- Basic familiarity with JavaScript

- Familiarity with a text editor, such as Notepad or SimpleText

Browser considerations: Cross-browser compatible site.

You'll use an external style sheet.

Here's how you should structure your site: Whenever you design a web site, it's best to start by planning the overall site structure and then planning the general layout of the pages in the site. The site structure is a map of the pages that will be included in the site, shown in a flowchart that indicates links between different pages.

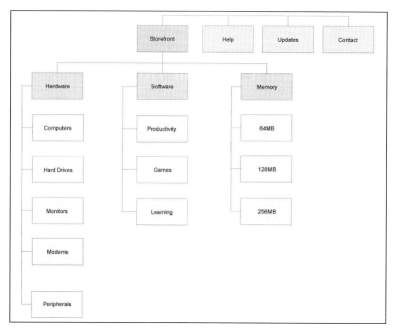

Use a flowchart to map out your site's structure.

The layout will generally be a graphic representation of the web page and its parts, which you can either hand-sketch or use a graphics-editing program, such as Photoshop.

How the site's architecture looks: With an e-commerce site, you must give special consideration to allowing your customers the ability to quickly find the items for which they are looking. Generally, this is done by breaking your inventory up into logical segments, so that the client is not inundated with long lists of products that include items for which they are not looking.

Incorporating style sheets: You'll work with a basic template and modify the template from that point.

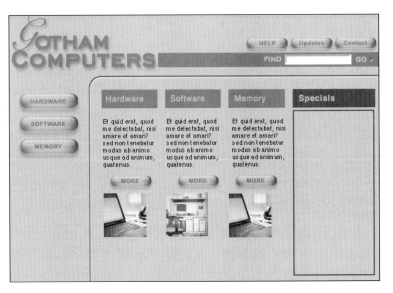

Use a program, such as Photoshop, to mock up your site's look (or you can sketch it by hand).

TAILORING YOUR CSS FOR THE BROWSER TYPE

Whenever you develop a web site for the masses, make it look as good as possible on the widest number of browsers. With CSS, you can actually include two or more external style sheets: one to set the optimal appearance and the others to tailor the appearance for a particular browser. You then use JavaScript to detect the browser and version, and add a link to the external CSS file to make corrections for that browser.

Listing 9.1 shows the default CSS settings for the web site. You can download the code from this book's web site, and begin to add the modifications that assist with interoperability.

LISTING 9.1   DEFAULT CSS SETTINGS

```
body {
    background-color: #99cc00;
    margin-top: 0px;
    margin-left: 5px;
}
p,td {
    font: 10px Arial, Helvetica, Geneva, sans-serif;
}
```

continues

continued

Note: Pixels or points—which should you use? This issue is being debated, with some insisting that point sizing is a more "traditional" method. An interesting article on the subject, called "Give Me Pixels or Give Me Death" can be found at www.alistapart.com/stories/fear4/index.html.

Personally, I recommend using pixels to define sizes for web pages and save point sizes for print needs, because point sizes do not display consistently between Mac and Windows operating systems. Windows tends to display fonts defined in points larger than the Mac. So, text set to 10pt may look fine in Windows, but be too small on a Mac.

```css
.buttonText {
    font-weight: bold;
    font-size: 14px;
    font-family: Arial, Helvetica, Geneva, sans-serif;
    margin-top: 0px;
    padding-top: 4px
}

.buttonTextSmall  {
    font-weight: bold;
    font-size: 10px;
    font-family: Arial, Helvetica, Geneva, sans-serif;
    margin-top: 0px;
    padding-top: 4px;
}

h2  {
    color: #660066;
    font: bold 24px Arial, Helvetica, Geneva, sans-serif;
}

h3 {
    color: #99cc00;
    font: bold 14px Arial, Helvetica, Geneva, sans-serif;
}

h4 {
    color: #660066;
    font: bold 12px Arial, Helvetica, Geneva, sans-serif;
}
```

To prepare your CSS for Netscape 4:

1 Open the file netscape4.css in the web site's Chapter09 folder and add the following:

This file holds the tweaks that you need to make to the CSS in order to have it appear optimally in Netscape 4.

```css
.buttonText  {
    margin-top: 4px;
    padding-top: 0px;
}
.buttonTextSmall  {
    margin-top: 4px;
    padding-top: 0px;
}
```

Test your work in Netscape 4 prior to the CSS correction to uncover problems with the way the page is displayed.

Add the CSS fix to allow proper positioning of `button` attributes in Netscape 4.

2 Open the file `index.html` (found on the web site) and, in the `<head>` of the document, add a link to `default.css`:

The default CSS is now used in this page.

```
<link href="css/default.css" rel="styleSheet" type="text/css">
```

3 Immediately after the `link` tag that you added in Step 3, add the following JavaScript:

This script tests the browser to see if it is Netscape 4. If it is, a second `link` tag is written into the `<head>` of the document. Now the CSS definitions from `netscape4.css` override the definitions of `default.css` and replace any redundant ones, which in this case, will be the top margin and top padding for the `buttonTextSmall` class.

```
<script language="JavaScript" type="text/javascript">
    if ((navigator.appName.indexOf('Netscape') !=
➡-1)&&(parseInt(navigator.appVersion)==4)) {
    document.write('<link href="css/netscape4.css" rel="styleSheet"
➡type="text/css">'); }
</script>
```

FIXING THE NETSCAPE 4 CSS BUG

Now that you have set up CSS for particular browsers, you also need to add a small JavaScript function to your web page to combat a major bug in Netscape that causes the browser to "lose" its formatting, if the visitor resizes the window. First, you have to tell the browser to be on the lookout if visitors resize their windows. If they do, you need to make the page reload, thus restoring CSS.

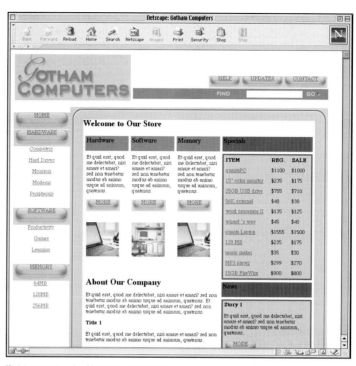

If visitors resize the Netscape 4 window, your page loses its formatting. This exercise corrects the problem.

1 Open the file `index.html` and replace the `<script>` container in the `<head>`:

```
<script language="JavaScript" type="text/javascript">
</script>
```

2 Within the `<script></script>` container, insert:

This tests for the browser's version and whether the window was resized or not.

```
if ((navigator.appName.indexOf('Netscape') !=
➡-1)&&(parseInt(navigator.appVersion)==4)) {
                    origWidth = innerWidth;
                    origHeight = innerHeight;
        }
```

Caution: Although many developers test by browser version, others point out that testing the *Document Object Model* (DOM) version is a much more accurate way of testing for a browser's capabilities. This is based on the way the browser is built, rather than the browser brand. An example of general DOM testing looks like this:

```
if (window.innerWidth != null)
{
    origWidth = innerWidth;
    origHeight = innerHeight;
}
```

As with many things in web design, developers make choices to use one method over another for numerous reasons. A popular reason to test for browsers by name is if there's a clear demographic of users visiting a specific site.

There is a problem with DOM detection in Netscape 4. If the DOM detection script is in an external .js file *and* if the HTML document is the first one loaded in the window, Netscape 4 fails. That's why I have reverted to browser detection for Netscape 4.

3 Within the `<script>` container, add this JavaScript function:

If resizing is detected, this function reloads the page.

```
function reloadPage() {
    if (innerWidth != origWidth || innerHeight != origHeight)
    location.reload();
}
```

4 Within the `<script>` container, insert the following:

The upshot is that, if your customer is using Netscape 4 and resizes their browser window is causing the CSS to disappear, the page is quickly reloaded and the CSS is restored. (See figure on the following page.)

```
    if ((navigator.appName.indexOf('Netscape') !=
➥-1)&&(parseInt(navigator.appVersion)==4))
onresize = reloadPage;
```

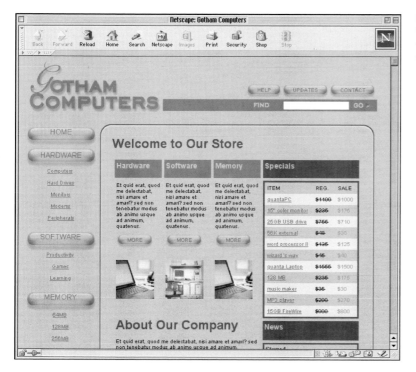

Instruct the browser to check for resizing. If it is detected, tell the page to reload and, thus, restore the CSS.

CREATING A LAYOUT GRID WITH TABLES

Although CSS has much to offer for creating web-page layout, the best way to create the overall layout of a page with columns is by using tables. I made this decision because it ensures that the complex visual structure of the site will remain intact across browsers, even though I'm using style sheets for the majority of the visual presentation.

In this section, you learn how to set up the basic layout structure of the Gotham Computers storefront web page by using tables:

1 Open the file `index.html` in the Chapter 9 folder on the web site.

You already linked the `default.css file` to this file (refer to Step 2 in the previous section, "Tailoring Your CSS for the Browser Type").

Note: Despite the power that style sheets can provide in terms of colors, fonts, margins, and other presentational features, many web designers and developers are still choosing to use tables as the grid on which their designs are built. This is because browsers have several insurmountable obstacles when it comes to interpreting CSS. Ultimately, CSS provides the most opportunity to separate presentation from content. However, the grid system that HTML tables provide is most consistent, stable, and predictable across a range of browsers.

2 In the <body> of the document, add the following

This sets up the basic table structure of the Gotham Computer's header—a table that's three rows tall by four columns wide.

Caution: In order for certain table attributes, such as background color to work, the table data cell must contain content even if that content is only a <br> tag.

```html
<table border="0" cellpadding="2" cellspacing="0" width="99%">
    <tr> <!-- Row 1 -->
        <td rowspan="3" width="270"><br></td>
        <td valign="bottom" align="right" height="66" colspan="3"><br></td>
    </tr>
    <tr> <!-- Row 2 -->
        <td valign="middle" class="buttonText" bgcolor="#577200" align="right"><br></td>
        <td valign="middle" bgcolor="#577200" align="right"><br></td>
        <td valign="middle" bgcolor="#577200" align="left" width="40"><br></td>
    </tr>
    <tr> <!-- Row 3 -->
        <td valign="top" align="right"><br></td>
        <td valign="top" align="right" ><br></td>
        <td valign="top" align="right" width="40"><br></td>
    </tr>
</table>
```

Create the table-based grid structure of the page.

3 Immediately after the header table, insert this markup:

This creates the menu and content columns of the page.

```html
<table border="0" cellpadding="0" cellspacing="2" width="100%">
    <tr>
        <!-- Menu Column -->
        <td width="150" valign="top" align="left"><br></td>
        <!-- Content Column -->
        <td width="100%" valign="top" align="left"><br></td>
    </tr>
</table>
```

Use tables to create the menu and content columns.

4 Insert the following table code into the content column's `<td>` container, creating the grid for the visual elements contained within the content column:

Tip: Using a table within a table is a technique referred to as *nesting tables*. Nesting tables is perfectly acceptable, although the more complex a table, the more a browser has to work to interpret the markup and thus the longer it will take to display the page. Therefore, limitations on nesting should be self-imposed. Nesting deeper than three times is usually a hint that a revised approach to your table is in order.

```
<table border="0" cellpadding="3" cellspacing="5" width="100%">
    <tr>
        <td width="100" bgcolor="#577200"><br></td>
        <td width="100" bgcolor="#577200"><br></td>
        <td width="100" bgcolor="#577200" ><br></td>
        <td width="100%" bgcolor="#660066"><br></td>
    </tr>
    <tr>
        <td width="100" valign="top"><br></td>
        <td width="100" valign="top"><br></td>
        <td width="100" valign="top"><br></td>
        <!-- Special Offers -->
        <td width="100%" valign="top" align="left" rowspan="2"><br></td>
    </tr>
    <tr>
        <td valign="top" colspan="3" rowspan="3"><br></td>
    </tr>
    <tr>
        <td width="100%" valign="top" align="left"
➥bgcolor="#660066"><br></td>
    </tr>
    <tr>
        <!-- News -->
        <td width="100%" valign="top" align="left"><br></td>
    </tr>
</table>
```

Nest a table within a table to create the grid upon which the content will reside. Note the addition of background color to specific cells.

5 Add the content to the page—in this case, the product heading:

```
<h3>Hardware</h3>
```

Make sure that you place your content within a <td> container. This ensures that the table cell won't collapse because the break is interpreted as content.

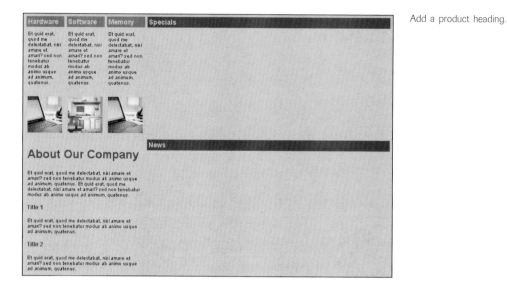

Add a product heading.

CREATING A SOLID BORDER

Some areas onscreen need to be separate from other onscreen areas. Creating distinctive and colorful headers for your document (without the need to resort to slow loading graphics) is possible using regular HTML text combined with a background color in a table cell. To do this, follow these steps:

1 In index.html, find the <td> container that's marked as special offers and add a background color attribute:

```
<!-- Special Offers -->
<td width="100%" valign="top" align="left" rowspan="2"
➥bgcolor="#660066"><br></td>
```

This action colors the entire cell a nice, deep purple, which will eventually become the border color.

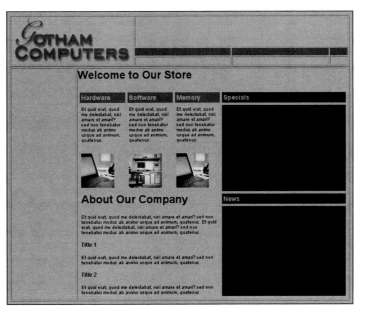

Add a background color attribute to the special offers table cell.

2 Within the `<td>` container, add a nested table that consists of one cell:

This creates a block of purple from which you'll in effect "knock out" the border.

```
<table border="0" cellpadding="3" cellspacing="0" width="100%">
    <tr>
        <td valign="top" align="left"><br></td>
    </tr>
</table>
```

3 Set the background color of the nested table to the background color of the page (green):

```
bgcolor="#99cc00"
```

Tip: If you want the border to be thicker, set a wider padding for the table.

4 Set the background color for the <td> labeled "News" to purple and copy the code from Steps 2 and 3 into it.

This sets up a border for the news area.

5 Add your content within the nested tables.

The great thing about this border is that it will stretch both horizontally and vertically to accommodate the content in the tables. However, if the content does not fill the available space, you might get a thicker border to the right or at the bottom. You can overcome that by adding a few extra <br> tags in the innermost table cell to fill the space.

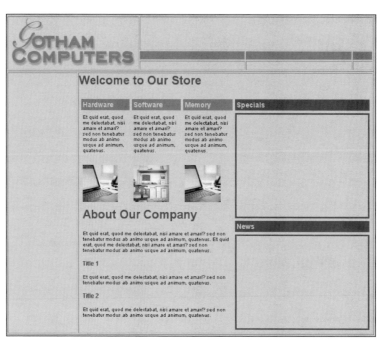

Create a border by nesting a table with a different background color than the main cell.

SETTING LINK APPEARANCE WITH CSS

Link colors highlight hypertext links on the page. With CSS you not only can set the color, but you can also set the font, size, and other CSS attributes of four different states (link, active, hover, and visited). Better yet, you can set multiple link styles in a single web page.

1 Open the file default.css in Chapter09/project/css folder on the web site, and insert this code to set the default appearance of a standard link:

```
a:link    {
        color: #336600;
        font-weight: bold;
        text-decoration: underline;
        background-color: transparent;
}
```

Set the attributes for an unvisited link.

2 After you define the link's appearance, insert the following code:

This sets the color and style of a visited link. That is, a link to a page that the vitor has already been to.

```
a:visited   {
        color: #336600;
        font-weight: normal;
        text-decoration: underline;
        background-color: transparent;
}
```

Computers

Set the attributes for a visited link.

3 After you set the appearance of the visited link, insert the following code:

This sets the appearance of the link when the customer has their mouse pointer over the link. To really make the link stand out before customers click it, invert the colors by setting the text to the light green used in the background and the background color as the dark green that's used in the link state. In addition, turn off the underlining and make the text bold.

```
a:hover   {
        color: #99cc00;
        font-weight: bold;
        text-decoration: none;
        background-color: #336600;
}
```

Computers

Set the attributes for a hover link.

Caution: The hover state is a nice alternative to using JavaScript rollovers, which require extra code and extra graphics. However, some browsers, such as Netscape 4, do not support hover state. Users accessing a page using hover with a browser that doesn't support the feature will still be able to see the link colors, but there will be no change to the link as the mouse passes over the link.

4 After you set the hover definition, insert the following code:

This describes your active link's features. An active link is the color a link will turn when the mouse clicks the link.

```
a:active  {
        color: #336600;
        font-weight: bold;
        text-decoration: none;
        background-color: transparent;
}
```

Computers

Set the attributes for an active link.

Note: In CSS, a special category is used to add special effects to a given selector. This category is referred to as a *pseudo-class*. Its syntax follows this format:

```
selector:pseudo-class {
    property: value;
}
```

In this section, I demonstrate pseudo-classes associated with the anchor <a> element. You can also use pseudo-classes and classes together, as I demonstrate in the additional link features that follow in this style sheet.

5 Insert this code after the active link pseudo-class:

This code adds additional link styles associated with a class called *button*. Now whenever a link is given the button class, it will use this appearance instead of the standard link apperance presented above. Notice that I combined pseudo-classes and standard classes. The a is the selector, the .button is a class, and the :effect_name_here is the pseudo-class.

```
a.button:link {
    color: #336600;
    text-decoration: none;
    background-color: transparent;
}
a.button:visited {
    color: #336600;
    text-decoration: none;
    background-color: transparent;
}
a.button:active {
    color: #336600;
    text-decoration: none;
    background-color: transparent;
}
a.button:hover {
    color: #558822;
    text-decoration: none;
    background-color: transparent;
}
```

Use classes and pseudo-classes to create button effects.

162

MODIFYING A GRAPHIC BUTTON WITH CSS

Graphic buttons are great for letting the visitor know to "click here" without having to say it. However, creating buttons means having to create a different graphic for every unique button in your web page. Add JavaScript rollovers to the equation, and that means at least two versions of every button adding up to a lot of graphics and a lot of download time. To streamline the process and reduce the overhead that this approach can produce, you can use CSS, HTML text, and a three graphics to make as many different buttons as you want. First, you need to have a graphic to work with. I created one in Photoshop. (See the sidebar, "Creating a Graphic Button" for details.) After I finished the graphic, I was able to add CSS to achieve my goals.

With your button graphic ready, you can add the CSS and HTML:

1   Open the file `buttonTest.html` in Chapter09/project on the companion web site.

    This is a blank HTML file linked to `default.css`. You can use this file to create your button and move it to `index.html` when it's ready.

CREATING A GRAPHIC BUTTON

In order to create the graphic button that's used in this section, I followed a number of steps. You can download the file called `button.gif` from this book's web site and try it yourself by using the imaging program of your choice, or simply study the individual pieces to see how I achieved my results.

First, I designed the entire button. Then I cut the left cap and center pieces, saving them to a subfolder called media. I named these files `buttonCapLeft.gif` and `buttonBG.gif`.

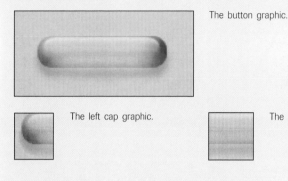

The button graphic.

The left cap graphic.

The Background Graphic.

Then I flipped the left cap graphic, named `buttonCapLeft.gif` horizontally to make the right cap graphic. I named this `buttonCapRight.gif` and saved it in the media folder.

The right cap graphic.

2 Insert the following code:

This action adds the button, and tightly controls the placement of its individual slices.

```
<table border="0" cellpadding="0" cellspacing="0">
    <!-- Button Begin -->
    <tr>
      <td><img src="media/buttonCapLeft.gif" width="30" height="36" border="0" alt=""></td>
      <td class="buttonText" valign="top" align="center" background="media/buttonBG.gif">
      <!-- Button Link Goes Here -->
      </td>
      <td><img src="media/buttonCapRight.gif" width="30" height="36" border="0" alt=""></td>
    </tr>
    <!-- Button End -->
</table>
```

The button table structure.

3 Insert the following markup in the center column:

This adds the actual link and button name.

```
<a class="button" href="#">HOME</a>
```

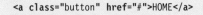

Create the final button.

4 Insert Listing 9.2 in the menu column of `index.html`:

LISTING 9.2   ADDING A MENU WITH MULTIPLE BUTTONS

```
<table border="0" cellpadding="0" cellspacing="0">
    <!-- Button Begin -->
    <tr>
      <td><img src="media/buttonCapLeft.gif" width="30" height="36" border="0" alt=""></td>
      <td class="buttonText" valign="top" align="center" background="media/buttonBG.gif"><a
➥class="button" href="#">HOME</a></td>
```

continues

```
      <td><img src="media/buttonCapRight.gif" width="30" height="36" border="0" alt=""></td>
    </tr>
    <!-- Button End -->
    <!-- Button Begin -->
    <tr>
      <td></td>
      <td class="buttonText" valign="top" align="center"></td>
      <td></td>
    </tr>
    <tr>
      <td><img src="media/buttonCapLeft.gif" width="30" height="36" border="0" alt=""></td>
      <td class="buttonText" valign="top" align="center" background="media/buttonBG.gif"><a class="button" href="#">HARDWARE</a></td>
      <td><img src="media/buttonCapRight.gif" width="30" height="36" border="0" alt=""></td>
    </tr>
    <!-- Button End -->
    <!-- Button Begin -->
    <tr>
      <td></td>
      <td valign="top" align="center"><a href="#">Computers</a>
        <p><a href="#">Hard Drives</a></p>
        <p><a href="#">Monitors</a></p>
        <p><a href="#">Modems</a></p>
        <p><a href="#">Peripherals</a></p>
        <p><br>
        </p>
      </td>
      <td></td>
    </tr>
    <tr>
      <td><img src="media/buttonCapLeft.gif" width="30" height="36" border="0" alt=""></td>
      <td class="buttonText" valign="top" align="center" background="media/buttonBG.gif"><a class="button" href="#">SOFTWARE</a></td>
      <td><img src="media/buttonCapRight.gif" width="30" height="36" border="0" alt=""></td>
    </tr>
    <!-- Button End -->
    <!-- Button Begin -->
    <tr>
      <td></td>
      <td valign="top" align="center"><a href="#">Productivity</a>
        <p><a href="#">Games</a></p>
        <p><a href="#">Learning</a></p>
        <p><br>
        </p>
      </td>
      <td></td>
    </tr>
    <tr>
      <td><img src="media/buttonCapLeft.gif" width="30" height="36" border="0" alt=""></td>
```

```
          <td class="buttonText" valign="top" align="center" background="media/buttonBG.gif"><a class="button" href="#">MEMORY</a></td>
          <td><img src="media/buttonCapRight.gif" width="30" height="36" border="0" alt=""></td>
        </tr>
        <tr>
          <td></td>
          <td valign="top" align="center"><a href="#">64MB</a>
            <p><a href="#">128MB</a></p>
            <p><a href="#">256MB</a></p>
          </td>
          <td></td>
        </tr>
        <!-- Button End -->
    </table>
```

This code adds the menu for the Gotham Computer web page. As you can see, the table is complex, but that complexity is part of what keeps each visual element of the page intact.

5 Load buttonCapLeft.gif, buttonCapRight.gif, and buttonBG.gif into a graphics program. Reduce their size by 25 percent, and resave them as buttonSmallCapLeft.gif, buttonSmallCapRight.gif, and buttonSmallBG.gif.

You can use these smaller versions of the buttons for the auxiliary links and more buttons.

Create the button menu.

6 Insert the following code into `index.html` to place the buttons:

Note: The `background` attribute doesn't work in most browsers prior to 4.0 versions. As such, you must be careful not to put critical information into the background unless you've considered your audience and made the decision to not support earlier browsers.

```
<table border="0" cellpadding="0" cellspacing="0">
    <tr>
        <!-- Button Begin -->
        <td valign="top" height="25">
            <img src="media/buttonSmallCapLeft.gif" width="21"
height="25" border="0">
        </td>
        <td align="center" background="media/buttonSmallBG.gif"
height="25" valign="top" class="buttonTextSmall">

            <a class="button" href="#">MORE</a>
        </td>
        <td valign="top" height="25">
            <img src="media/buttonSmallCapRight.gif" width="21"
height="25" border="0">
        </td>
        <!-- Button End -->
    </tr>
</table>
```

Place a small button onto the page.

FORMATTING TEXT FROM A DATABASE

When you create a site that relies on input from a database, you never know exactly how that content will be presented. It might be in all lowercase, uppercase, or a combination of both. Using CSS, you can ensure that the content drawn from a database is presented correctly:

1 Open `default.css` and insert the following code:

In this case, you're ensuring that any text information delivered from a database will be displayed in a table cell with a background color of #99FF66 in all caps.

```
td.database1 {
    background-color: #99ff66;
    text-transform: capitalize;
}
td.database2 {
    text-transform: capitalize;
}
```

2 While you're still in `default.css`, insert the following code:

```
.regPrice {
    text-decoration: line-through;
}
.salePrice {
    color: red;
}
```

3 In `index.html`, insert the following code in the Sales area, replacing the nested table that's currently there:

Specials		
ITEM	**REG.**	**SALE**
QuantaPC	$~~1100~~	$1000
15" Color Monitor	$~~235~~	$175
25GB USB Drive	$~~755~~	$710
56K External	$~~40~~	$38
Word Processor II	$~~135~~	$125
Wizard 'S Way	$~~45~~	$40
Quanta Laptop	$~~1555~~	$1500
128 MB	$~~235~~	$175
Music Maker	$~~35~~	$30
MP3 Player	$~~299~~	$270
15GB FireWire	$~~900~~	$800

Create the special items list.

```html
<table border="0" cellpadding="5" cellspacing="0" width="100%"
bgcolor="#99cc00">
    <tr>
        <td valign="top" align="left"><b>ITEM</b></td>
        <td valign="top" align="left"><b>REG.</b></td>
        <td valign="top" align="left"><b>SALE</b></td>
    </tr>
    <tr>
        <td class="database1" valign="top" align="left"><a
➥href="#">quantaPC</a></td>
        <td class="database1" valign="top" align="left"><span
➥class="regPrice">$1100</span></td>
        <td class="database1" valign="top" align="left"><span
➥class="salePrice">$1000</span></td>
    </tr>
    <tr>
        <td class="database2" valign="top" align="left"><a
➥href="#">15&quot; color monitor</a></td>
        <td class="database2" valign="top" align="left"><span
➥class="regPrice">$235</span></td>
        <td class="database2" valign="top" align="left"><span
➥class="salePrice">$175</span></td>
    </tr>
</table>
```

ADDING A SEARCH FORM

Although the menu offers one way of finding items, many customers will want to search the products by typing in one or more keywords. Although showing you how to create a search engine for an entire site falls outside this book's scope, adding a Search field and Submit button are relatively simple tasks:

1 Open the file index.html and add the following code immediately before the header table:

This sets up the form and how it will behave.

```
<form name="FormName" action="#" method="post">
```

Note: You need to check with your ISP to find out the proper action and method values. These differ according to the type of server your web page is sitting on and what application is being used to generate forms.

2 Insert the input field in the third column, second row of the header table:

```
<input type="text" name="searchCriteria" size="20">
```

3 Insert the Submit button in the fourth column, second row of the header table:

```
<input type="image" src="media/searchGo.gif" width="38" height="18" border="0">
```

4 Insert the closing form tag immediately after the header table in index.html:

```
</form>
```

Note: The width, height, and border attributes in the input element will not validate in HTML of XHTML. You can leave them out if you prefer.

Design an attractive search form.

MORE MAGIC

Borders can help guide the eye to discrete areas of important information. Earlier in this chapter, you used table cell color to create a border. But, two other methods of creating borders are important to mention.

Creating Graphic Borders

Although the solid border created in this chapter is easy to set up, you can only control the border color and thickness. You can create your own unique border by using graphics within a table. However, to add this border, you need to retool the table you created in Step 3 of the section, "Creating a Layout Grid with Tables."

1 Open the file `border.gif`, which is located in Chapter09/project/graphics.

This graphic contains all the elements needed to create the border: the four corners and four sides. I created this graphic in Photoshop.

Open the file `border.gif`.

2 Open your imaging program, preferably Photoshop. Cut the top-left corner, top side, and left-side graphics. Save each piece as GIFs with the names `borderCapTL.gif`, `borderTop.gif`, and `borderLeft.gif`, respectively, in the media folder.

Slice the graphic into separate pieces: `borderCapTL.gif`.

`borderLeft.gif`.

`borderTop.gif`.

3 Flip the graphics from Step 2 to make the other corner and side graphics:

- Flip `borderCapTL.gif` *horizontally* to create the top-right corner. Save this as `media/borderCapTR.gif`.

- Flip `borderCapTR.gif` *vertically* to create the bottom-right corner. Save this as `media/borderCapBR.gif`.

Flip the graphics: `borderCapTR.gif`.

`borderCapBR.gif`.

`borderCapBL.gif`.

`borderRight.gif`.

`borderCapBottom.gif`.

- Flip borderCapBR.gif *horizontally* to create the bottom-left corner. Save this as media\borderCapBR.gif.

- Flip borderLeft.gif *horizontally* to create the right side. Save this as media\borderRight.gif.

- Flip borderTop.gif *vertically* to create the bottom side. Save this as media\borderBottom.gif.

4 Replace the table you added in step 3 of the section, "Creating a Layout Grid with Tables" with the version in Listing 9.3.

This version of the content table adds two additional rows and two additional columns to accommodate the graphic border. The graphics are inserted around the central content column cell. The corners are inserted directly into the corner cells while the sides are set as backgrounds on each of the side cells, so that they stretch to accommodate the content cell. In addition, the menu column now needs to stretch across three rows. Refer to the sidebar, "Creating a Graphic Button" for more details.

LISTING 9.3   ADDING THE BUTTON SLICES TO AN HTML TABLE

```html
<table border="0" cellpadding="0" cellspacing="0" width="99%">
    <tr>
        <!-- Menu Column -->
        <td width="150" valign="top" align="left" rowspan="3"><br></td>
        <td width="29" valign="top" align="left"><img
➥src="../media/borderCapTL.gif" width="29" height="27" border="0"></td>
        <td width="100%" valign="top" align="left"
➥background="../media/borderTop.gif"><br></td>
        <td width="29" valign="top" align="left"><img
➥src="../media/borderCapTR.gif" width="29" height="27" border="0"></td>
    </tr>
    <tr>
        <td width="29" valign="top" align="left"
➥background="../media/borderLeft.gif"><br></td>
        <!-- Content Column -->
        <td width="100%" valign="top" align="left">
        <!-- Place the nest table in here -->
    </td>
        <td width="29" valign="top" align="left"
➥background="../media/borderRight.gif"><br></td>
    </tr>
    <tr>
        <td width="29" valign="top" align="left"><img
➥src="../media/borderCapBL.gif" width="29" height="27" border="0"></td>
        <td width="100%" valign="top" align="left"
➥background="../media/borderBottom.gif"><br></td>
        <td width="29" valign="top" align="left"><img
➥src="../media/borderCapBR.gif" width="29" height="27" border="0"></td>
    </tr>
</table>
```

View the bordered table structure.

Create the graphic table border.

(Re)insert the nested column from step 4 in the section, "Creating a Layout Grid with Tables" in the content column.

CSS Borders

CSS offers several cool border options through the border property. This property is a shorthand property that defines the width, color, and style of a border. Here's an example:

```
div {
    border: 2px dashed blue;
}
```

This means that any element using the div element will appear with a two-pixel, dashed blue border.

Border styles include dotted, dashed, solid, double, groove, ridge, inset, and outset. Try them out for yourself—but be certain that you're using a browser that can properly interpret your choices. For the most up-to-date information on browser support for CSS, see www.webreview.com/style/css1/charts/mastergrid.shtml.

"A helping word to one in trouble is often like

a switch on a railroad track…an inch between

wreck and smooth-rolling prosperity."

—HENRY WARD BEECHER

PROVIDING ONLINE CUSTOMER SUPPORT

Just about any study is almost unaminous,

in part because E-commerce web sites fail

because users get confused, discouraged, and

tend to leave if they can't quickly find the

information that they want. Often, the web

site's overall interface is the chief culprit.

Interface designers must balance the needs of

experienced and first-time users. Experienced

users know where they are going and want to

access the quickest route with the minimum fuss,

while "newbies" need more hand holding. So,

how do you simultaneously allow experienced

users the flexibility they desire without alienating

new users?

Providing Online Customer Support

By Jason Cranford Teague

The final Help page offers several different avenues for users to find answers and guidance.

The answer? Provide a clear Help page for new users. Help pages are often overlooked until the end of a project and are forced into the interface right before the site launches. However, the Help page might be one of the most critical parts of a web site—especially for new web sites where every user is new. If you revisit Chapter 9, "Setting Up a Storefront," and look at the figure that illustrates the project's outcome, you'll see that the Help section was designed into the interface early on, anticipating the user's need. In this chapter, you look carefully at how to implement the planned-for Help section.

PROJECT SNAPSHOT

The problem: Your site users have differing levels of skills. The goal is to have the users enjoy your site and use it easily. How can you help them?

Who this chapter is for: Having a specialized Help section empowers your users by providing information on the best ways to use your site and any of it's special features. This, in turn, inspires the occasional visitor to become a regular one.

TECHNICAL SPECS

The following are the technical specifications that you need:

- **Markup used**—HTML 4.01
- *Document type definition* (**DTD**) **used**—Transitional

Here are the additional technologies or skills that you need:

- Familiarity with HTML
- Basic familiarity with JavaScript
- Familiarity with a text editor, such as Notepad or SimpleText

Browser considerations: Cross-browser compatible site.

Style sheets: You'll use an external style sheet.

Structuring the site: The most important issue is to be sure to *plan* the Help page as part of your site's primary structure.

How the site's architecture looks: As I mentioned in Chapter 9, e-commerce sites should give special consideration to allowing customers the ability to quickly find the items for which they are looking. Whether it's product information or concerns about security features, having some information to help your visitors should be worked into the commerce site plan.

Incorporating style sheets: The site uses a basic template (which is found in Chapter 9) with modifications that you added as you worked through that chapter.

To set up your Help page, you need to use a template based on Chapter 9's e-commerce web site. You can find the template in Chapter 10's folder on this book's web site.

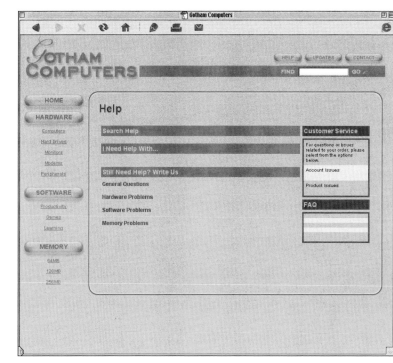

Use the template page to create your Help page.

FORMATTING SEARCH FIELDS

Most web designers know that *Cascading Style Sheets* (CSS) can format text's appearance in a web page. What you might not know, however, is that CSS can also control the appearance of form input elements on the screen. A form element is made up of three primary components: the border, text field, and text.

CSS enables us to control the appearance and color of the border, as well as the background for the field and the text style. Unfortunately, Netscape 4 doesn't support CSS applied to form elements. Although Netscape 6 seems to support CSS with forms to a certain degree, it is a bit quirky. However, using the techniques shown in this section will not interfere with these browsers.

Gotham Computers wants to tailor the look of the Search field for the Help screen to better integrate with the look and feel of the site. To do this, you must set up a class that defines the appearance of form fields:

1 Open the file `default.css` in Chapter 10's folder on the web site.

This file includes all the CSS code that you set up in Chapter 9.

2 Add the following code to `default.css`:

Use CSS to control the appearance of a form field's border, text field, and text.

```
input.searchField    {
     font-size: 12px;
     font-family: "Trebuchet MS", Arial, Helvetica, Geneva, sans-serif;
     background-color: #99ff66;
     border: solid 2px #577200;
}
```

Note: Many readers might be familiar with the concept of web-safe color. This is the technique of using the 216 colors that have been deemed more-or-less consistent across browsers and an individual's hardware (including a video card and a monitor). But many arguments have been made that the web-safe color is really not so safe. What's more, most people who are using browsers capable of interpreting CSS probably have computer systems with more sophisticated color management. As such, many designers decide to use colors outside of the safe palette. The decision to use "unsafe" colors is a perfectly acceptable one, if designers think through the issue and determine that their audiences are likely to accommodate those colors.

For a detailed article on this issue, see Molly's Web Techniques column, *Integrated Design*, May 2001. The online version of the article is available at `www.webtechniques.com/archives/2001/05/desi/`.

This code sets up a class called `searchField`, which can be applied to `<input>` tags only. Any `<input>` tag that includes the `searchField` class will display with a solid dark-green border that's 2 pixels wide. In addition, the background color of the field will be light green, and any text in the field will display at 12 pixels in one of the sans-serif fonts listed, depending on availability.

3 Save your changes and close this file.

Because `searchField` is a class, none of these definitions will be used until you set up an `input` field with the class defined as `searchField`.

4 Open the file `index.html` in Chapter 10's folder on this book's web site.

5 Insert search form code after comment:

This code sets up a simple search form field that will be used when finding information in the Help area. The text-input field indicates that it must use the `searchField` class to define its appearance.

Note: You are not limited to just adding a solid border around the text-input field. CSS has several other border types including dotted, dashed, double, groove, ridge, outset, and inset.

```
<form name="helpSearchForm" action="#" method="get">
<h4>Find</h4>
<input class="searchField" type="text" name="textfieldName"
➥size="24" tabindex="1">
<input type="image" src="media/searchGo.gif" align="top">
</form>
```

View the form field without CSS formatting.

Add CSS to give your form field a more controlled look.

DROP-DOWN MENU

One of my chief gripes about web sites is the overabundance of unorganized links strewn about the page. You've probably seen sites with long lists of links that stretch off of the window. They often add visual noise to the design and waste precious screen space without actually assisting with navigation. Drop-down menus are my preferred solution.

Gotham Computers is using the form `select` element to create a drop-down menu to help customers quickly find information about a specific topic. The customer will select one of the topics from the drop-down menu and instantly be taken to the relevant page.

To Create a drop down menu:

1 Open the file `default.css` and add the following:

This sets up a style to control the appearance of the form drop-down menu, as shown in the previous section. Select form fields have a solid dark-green border 2 pixels wide and a light-green background. The text will appear in one of the sans-serif fonts listed as available on the end-user's computer.

```
select {

    font-size: 12px;
    font-family: "Trebuchet MS", Arial, Helvetica, Geneva, sans-serif;
    background-color: #99ff66; border: solid 2px #577200;
}
```

2 Save this file and close it.

3 Open the file `index.html` in Chapter 10's folder on this book's web site. In the `<head>` of the document, add a `<script>` container:

You're getting ready to set up the drop-down menu. The code in Steps 4–7 will be added into this container.

```
<script language="JavaScript" type= text/JavaScript">

</script>
```

4 Add the following code into the `<script>` container from Step 3:

This defines the name of the page, which will come in handy later when you need to target links.

```
self.name='content';
```

5 Add the following code into the `<script>` container:

This sets up a function that's used to create *arrays*. An array is a variable that holds a list of things. In this case, you will use it in Step 6 to set up a list of URLs that are being accessed from your drop-down menu. An important note: Arrays begin numbering with 0, rather than 1. So the first item in an array list is referenced as 0, *not* 1.

```
function MakeArray() {
    this.length = MakeArray.arguments.length
    for (var i = 0; i < this.length; i++)
        this[i] = MakeArray.arguments[i]
}
```

6 Create the array to hold the list of URLs for the drop-down menu by adding the following code to the `<script>` container:

This array uses the function that you added in Step 5 to create a list of URLs recorded in the array `menuUrl[]`. Four items in the list are in the same order that their options will appear in the final menu (see Step 8). Notice that the first item in the list is blank. The first item in the menu will not be a link, but a single line of instructions. Thus, it does not need a URL associated with it.

```
var menuUrl = new MakeArray(
'',
'helpComputers.html',
'helpSoftware.html',
'helpMemory.html');
```

7 Add the `menuSelect()` function:

This JavaScript function uses the name of the form, passed to it as the variable `formName`, to look and see which option is currently selected. If the selected item is not the first item in the list (0), the function loads the corresponding URL from the `menuUrl[]` array into the window named `content` (from Step 4). Having the function is not enough, however. You need to set up a link to trigger it.

```
function menuSelect(formName) {
    i = formName.topic.selectedIndex;
    if (i == 0) return;
    else top.open(menuUrl[i],'content');
}
```

8 After the comment

`<!-- Add Drop Down Code Here -->`

add the following:

```
<form name="helpWith">
    <select name="topic" size="1" tabindex="2" onchange="menuSelect(this.form)">
        <option>Select One</option>
        <option>Computers</option>
        <option>Software</option>
        <option>Memory</option>
    </select>
</form>
```

Finally, you are adding the `<select>` form field to the page. This sets up a select box with four options. The first option simply tells the user what to do, while the remaining three options correspond to topics where the user can find more information.

Also notice that the `<select>` tag includes the JavaScript event handler `onChange`. When one of the options is selected, the function `menuSelect()` runs. For example, if the customer selects the second item in the drop-down list, the second URL in the array opens. The upshot? When the user selects one of the last three options, the corresponding topic page is loaded into the current window.

9 Save your work and load this page into a browser to view the results.

Keep in mind, however, that the URLs that you set up in Step 5 need to actually exist for the menu to work.

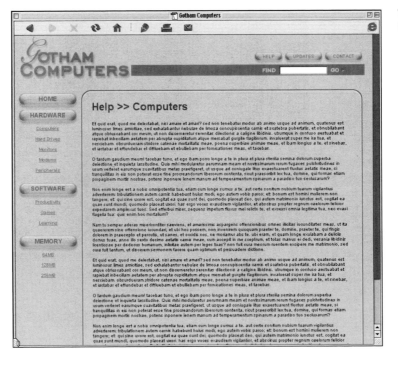

Prepare to use the drop-down menu.

Select the Software option that you just created.

Note: You can add as many menu options as you want to this menu, but remember that each option needs a corresponding URL in the `menuURL` array that you set up in Step 6.

View the Software information page.

FAQs: Anchoring Questions to Answers

A list of *Frequently Asked Questions* (FAQs) is a standard way of helping customers find the information for which they are looking. One problem with FAQs is that the list of questions and answers can get exceedingly long. Users want to be able to skim the list of questions to find the one that's closest to their own and then be taken to that question's answer.

On its Help page, Gotham Computers set up a list of the top questions they hear, but the answers are on another page. So Gotham not only needs to link to the Answer page, but also needs to anchor the link to the specific question/answer on the page. In addition, Gotham wants to format the Answers page so that each question and answer stands out by placing a large "Q" next to questions and a large "A" next to the answer.

1 Open the `default.css` file and add the following:

This creates two new classes: `question` and `answer`, respectively. `question` will be used to create the large Q and `answer`, obviously, will be used to create the large A. These classes are almost identical. However, the A must be drop cap, so the `answer` class needs to float to the left.

```css
.question {
    color: #577200;
    font-size: 36px;
    line-height: 36px;
    font-family: "Times New Roman", Georgia, Times, serif;
    text-align: center;
    float: none;
    clear: none;
    margin: 2px;
}

.answer {
    float: left;
    clear: none;
}
```

2 Open the file `index.html`. After the comment line add

`<!-- Add first FAQ Link Here -->`

Immediately after the note, add the following HTML link:

```html
<a href="helpFAQ.html#q5">
When will my order arrive?
</a>
```

This link not only opens `helpFAQ.html`, but it also moves the page down to the anchor q5. You can add as many different FAQs as you want to this list; just make sure that each one is anchored to a different answer in `helpFAQ.html`.

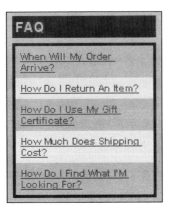

Using the list of FAQs about this web site.

3 Open the file `helpFAQ.html` (located in Chapter 10's folder). After the comment

`<!-- Insert Questions and Answers Here -->`

add the following:

This creates the anchor called q5 that the link set up in Step 2 looks for in this page. If there's enough room, the browser positions the page so that this anchor appears at the top of the screen. If the anchor did not exist, however, the page would simply load with the top of the page at the top of the screen. The effect is that the content underneath, in this case, your question and answer, will be drawn to the top of the screen, along with the anchor tag.

```
<p><a name="q5"></a></p>
```

Note: Notice that, at the bottom of the code for this page, a few dozen `<br>` tags exist. The anchor tag will always try to appear as close to the top of the page as possible. However, the browser will not add space at the bottom of the page to accommodate the anchor.

So if there's not enough content under the anchor tag, the question and answer will appear only part of the way up the screen and not at the very top. This is often confusing to users who expect the question and answer to appear at the top of the screen. The user might have to search around for a while to find the answer that she is looking for or she might not even realize that the answer is on the page. The `<br>` tags at the bottom of the page ensure that there will always be enough room for even the last question in the list to appear at the top of the screen.

4 Add the question immediately after the anchor link from Step 3:

The Q is surrounded by a `<span>` tag that's using the `question` class so that the Q will appear big and green next to the question.

```
<p>
<span class="question">Q</span>
<b>When will my order arrive?</b>
<br clear="all">
</p>
```

5 Add the answer to the question immediately after the code in Step 4:

Like the Q, the A will appear big and green next to the text for the answer, but the text of the answer will flow around it.

```
<p>
<span class="answer">A</span>
It will be coming very soon. Just wait.
</p>
```

6 For each question in your FAQ list in index.html, repeat Steps 3 to 5, and change the anchor name in Step 3 for each.

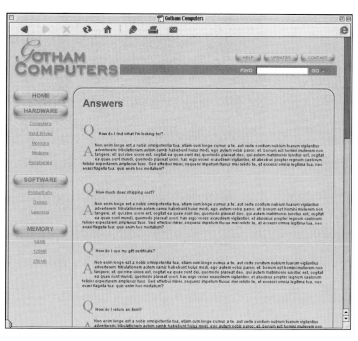

Refine the answer page.

POP-UP HELP WINDOWS

Pop-up windows allow you to present additional content in a new, smaller window without having to unload the content in the main window. This is especially useful for online help where you might need to explain how to use a specific page in greater detail than the page's space allows.

Gotham Computers will use pop-up windows to allow users to view additional help information without having to actually leave the Help page.

1 Add the function `helpOpen()` to the JavaScript in the head of `index.html`:

This function opens a new window that's 400 × 250 pixels wide by using the URL passed to it in the variable `fileName` and forces this new window to the front of the screen. You can change the sizes to meet your needs. Next, you need to include a link to activate the function.

```
function helpOpen(fileName) {
    customerService =
➥window.open(fileName,'customerService','width=400,height=250');
    window.customerService.focus();
}
```

2 After the comment

```
<!-- Insert Pop-up Window Links Here -->
```

add the following HTML link:

When the user clicks the link, the `helpOpen()` function is executed, opening a new window with the URL `helpAccInfo.html` as its source. You can use any URL that you want in its place. Now that you have the link set up to open the window, it's time to create the content to go in it.

```
<p><a href="javascript:helpOpen('helpAccInfo.html')">My Account Information</a></p>
```

3 Open the file `helpAccInfo.html` (located in Chapter10's folder).

This file will display content in the pop-up window and can thus contain anything you want. However, one problem users often complain about is that pop-up windows are confusing, especially if they click back to the main window. To overcome this, you must force the pop-up window to close itself once the visitor leaves.

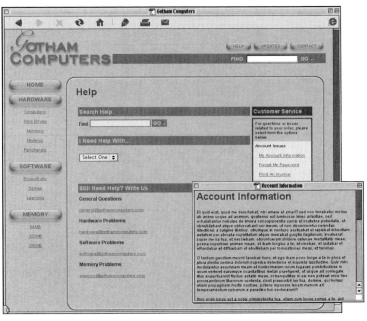

View the links to the pop-up windows.

Click a link and the pop-up window appears.

4 Add the following code to the `<body>` tag of `helpAccInfo.html`:

```
onblur="self.close()"
```

"Blur" means that the window is no longer selected. So when the window isn't selected (onBlur), the window closes itself. This will happen if the user clicks back to the original window.

ADDING A SUBJECT TO A MAILTO LINK

Mailto links are a common way of allowing visitors to quickly send an email from a web page by clicking a normal HTML link. The user clicks the link and the browser opens a new email in the user's default email program with the To address already filled in. You can also add a subject to this letter, which helps you tell from where in the site the user sent a particular email.

Gotham Computers will be using the mailto link to allow customers to send emails to a specific department within the company and include a predefined subject to let them know the contents of the email.

1 Open index.html. After the comment

`<!-- Add email link here -->`

add a link using the mail-to method

This looks like a standard HTML link, except that the URL begins with mailto and includes an email address rather than a web page's location. In addition, immediately after the email address, there's a question mark (?) and a subject for the email (in this case, General Question). You can replace this with anything you want.

```
<p>
<a href="mailto:general@gothamcomputers.com?subject=General
➥Question">general@gothamcomputers.com</a>
</p>
```

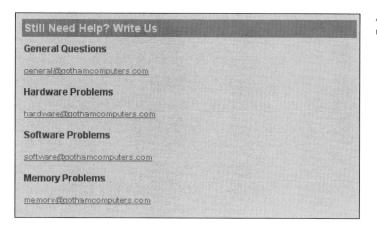

Still Need Help? Write Us

General Questions

general@gothamcomputers.com

Hardware Problems

hardware@gothamcomputers.com

Software Problems

software@gothamcomputers.com

Memory Problems

memory@gothamcomputers.com

Add a link by using the mail-to method.

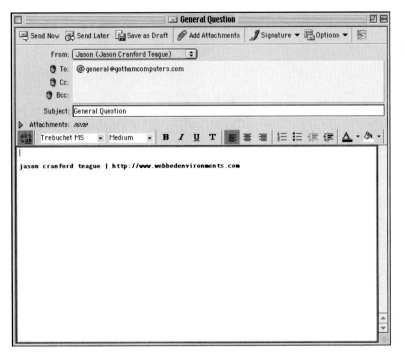

Click the link and your email client will open. Now you can compose an email that's ready to be sent to Gotham Computers.

MORE MAGIC

Naturally, some guidelines exist for writing help information. Try these on for size:

- Add descriptive information regarding general site-use information, such as preferred browsers and any necessary plug-ins (provide links to them, too).

- It's especially helpful on e-commerce sites to provide security information about how credit cards are processed and any other information that pertains to transactions and online legal purchases.

- A great technique for creating FAQs is to keep reader feedback on hand. Any prevalent concerns can be added to the existing FAQs over time. In general, a site needs to respond to its users' needs. If more than one person is experiencing difficulty with an aspect of your site's usability, it's good business to address those concerns.

Alternative Color Naming in CSS

Much of the color in this project was generated by using CSS and hexadecimal color. However, you can also use RGB color or color names.

To use RGB color, write the individual red, green, and blue values of the color, separated by commas:

```
color: rgb(0,0,255);
```

The resulting color is blue because red and green have no numeric values.

You can also use percentages of RGB:

```
color: rgb(100%,0%,0%);
```

In this case, the resulting color is pure red because it is at full percentage, while the green and blue colors are set to a 0 value.

Another option that you can use is the color name. CSS defines 16 total names: aqua, black, blue, fuchsia, gray, green, lime, maroon, navy, olive, purple, red, silver, teal, white, and yellow. You can use any of these names with your CSS:

```
color: lime
```

Some browsers are capable of reading proprietary names, but these 16 names are the only ones actually written into the *World Wide Web Consortium* (W3C) current recommendations for CSS.

"Paranoia means having all the facts."

—WILLIAM S. BORROUGHS

CREATING AN INFORMATION- BASED SITE

Information is the lifeblood of the web. No matter what else you might use the web for, information is always a part of everyone's online buffet. What's more, people that use wireless devices are almost always interested in finding information quickly and cleanly.

So how do you make a great information site for your web and wireless visitors? Well, resources and methods are available to help you. This chapter gets you going.

Project 10

Creating an Information-Based Site

By Christopher Schmitt

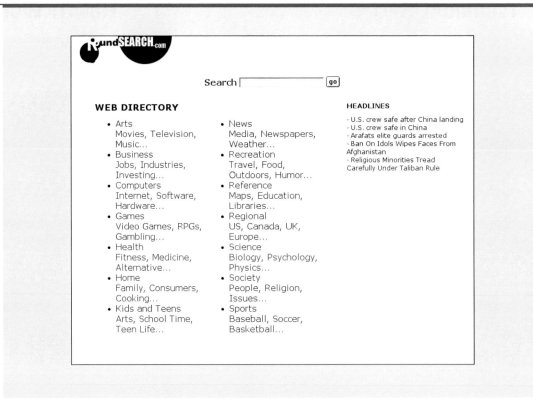

PROJECT SNAPSHOT

The problem: This section is about laying out pages without using the HTML table tags. Using *Cascading Style Sheets* (CSS), you can create a two-column layout that can still be used for hand-held devices or browsers without the proper CSS support.

This chapter is for anyone looking to lay out information-heavy web sites that provide numerous functions that are often competing for users' attention.

Technical Specs

The following are the technical specs that you need to use to create an information-based web site:

- **Markup used**—HTML 4, CSS, and JavaScript
- *Document type definitions* **(DTD) used**—HTML 4 transitional DTD

In this site's case, HTML 4 transitional was chosen because it is likely to be the best example for professionals that currently work to create information-based sites.

Here are the additional technologies or skills that you might need:

- Familiarity with HTML
- Basic familiarity with JavaScript
- Basic familiarity with CSS
- Familiarity with a text editor, such as Notepad or SimpleText

Finally, you will need a standards-compliant browser that renders HTML, JavaScript, and CSS properly.

Structuring the Site

When you set up an information source, it's not the structure of the site, but the structure of each page and how you create a jumping-off point for the information that's important. This means that you must create a variety of ways for people to get the information they require, but manage to keep the structure sensible.

Note: An information-rich web site must have multiple paths to the same information.

How It Works

To create a great information-based site, you will begin by designing a page layout with CSS in a two-column approach.

Tables are great elements for a web site because they allow designers to perform a grid layout of sorts—putting content chunks into separate areas around a web page. If you view existing web pages that have sidebars of left-hand navigation, or right-hand columns of ad banners, you are probably viewing a page that's been laid out with HTML tables.

With CSS, you can apply the design to the basic content and still be able to save the content for devices such as hand-held devices. At this time, limited graphical display and limited HTML support are hindrances for the portable digital assistants.

Remember the discussion in Chapter 1, "About Web Markup: XML, HTML, XHTML," about the separation of formatting and content? Well, this chapter shows you how to rely on style rather than tables for layout, which is a smart move—particularly when you develop sites that will be accessed by a variety of user agents.

Designing a Page Layout

The site that you will create, called Roundsearch, is a simple web-search directory that takes advantage of the Open Directory Project from dmoz.org and news headlines from Moreover.com. The first step to create this site is to acquire the content and format it into a typical top-to-bottom page layout.

Open Directory Project (ODP) is an online directory of web sites, much like Yahoo!. The nifty part about ODP is that the content is available for inclusion in your web site. You need to be able to set up a system that can pull the content into your web site.

Various scripts allow you to include the data either dynamically or with a cached version of the entire directory.

ODP++ (www.portalscripts.com/home/Free_Portal_Tools/ ODP__/odp__.shtml>) is a script that retrieves information from the directory on the fly, so you don't have to store the entire web directory on your server

You can use the ODP++ script to retrieve information from the Open Directory Project on the fly.

For headlines, Moreover.com delivers up-to-the-minute news that covers regional stories from sports to international events. Moreover.com supplies content in over 12 formats—XML to JavaScript to simple links for inclusion in your web site.

You can acquire content from Moreover.com to use on your web site.

Of course, don't forget the weather! HAMWeather.com provides two free scripts that provide weather information from the National Weather Service and Interactive Weather Information Network.

To layout your site, you'll start by organizing the information headings:

1 In a word processor or a simple text editor, place the information headings and content placeholders in order of importance.

The layout that I prefer for the Roundsearch site is

Roundsearch

    Search form internal link

    Web Directory internal link

    News Headlines internal link

    Search form

    Web Directory Header

    Content of Web Directory

    Headlines Header

    Content for Hews Headlines

2 Transfer this information into simple HTML:

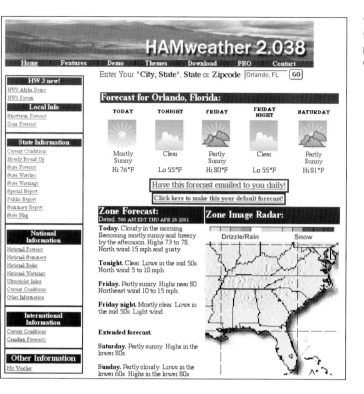

You can use the free scripts from **HAMWeather.com** to provide weather information on your site.

```
<!DOCTYPE HTML PUBLIC "-//W3C//DTD HTML 4.01 Transitional
➥//EN" "http://www.w3.org/TR/html4/loose.dtd"><html>

<head>
<title> information site </title>
</head>

<body>

<h1>Roundsearch</h1>

<ul>
```

continues

continued

```
<li><a href="#search">Search form</a>
<li><a href="#directory">Web Directory</a>
<li><a href="#headlines">News Headlines</a>
</ul>

<p><a name="search">Search form</a></p>

<h3><a name="directory">Web Directory Header</a></h3>

<p>Content of Web Directory</p>

<h3><a name="headlines">Headlines Header</a></h3>

<p>Content for Hews Headlines</p>

</body>
</html>
```

RoundSEARCH.com

Search [   ] [go]

WEB DIRECTORY

- Arts
  Movies, Television, Music...
- Business
  Jobs, Industries, Investing...
- Computers
  Internet, Software, Hardware...
- Games
  Video Games, RPGs, Gambling...
- Health
  Fitness, Medicine, Alternative...
- Home
  Family, Consumers, Cooking...
- Kids and Teens
  Arts, School Time, Teen Life...

- News
  Media, Newspapers, Weather...
- Recreation
  Travel, Food, Outdoors, Humor...
- Reference
  Maps, Education, Libraries...
- Regional
  US, Canada, UK, Europe...
- Science
  Biology, Psychology, Physics...
- Society
  People, Religion, Issues...
- Sports
  Baseball, Soccer, Basketball...

HEADLINES

- U.S. crew safe after China landing
- U.S. crew safe in China
- Arafats elite guards arrested
- Ban On Idols Wipes Faces From Afghanistan
- Religious Minorities Tread Carefully Under Taliban Rule

Set up the site in simple HTML with no style applied.

HIDING THE TABLE OF CONTENTS

The next step to creating an information-based web site is to go through the HTML
and change the code to enhance the presentation using CSS:

1 Replace

```
<h1>Roundsearch</h1>
```

with the following:

```
<img src="logo.gif" alt="Roundsearch — Main Page" width="150"
►height="60">
```

Replacing the heading of the page and with a logo image brands the site. Restricting the image width to 150 pixels or less ensures that hand-held devices can render the image on the small screen.

2 Insert the `class` attribute `toc` in the unordered list tag, `ul`:

The `toc` attribute stands for table of contents. The style sheet you create in Step 3 uses it to make the table of contents invisible. Typically, having a table of contents or a site map is necessary so your visitors can navigate through the pages more easily. However, because the content will be mostly visible in the top-most section of the document (and, therefore, the most immediately visible), you can hide it from view.

```
<ul class="toc">
```

3 Between the `head` tags, start to build the style sheet:

In the style sheet, you reference the unordered list with the `.toc` selector and declare the display to be set to none, or invisible. But have no fear, the table of contents still exists if your browser doesn't render CSS.

```
<style type="text/css">
<!--

.toc {
        display: none;
}

-->
</style>
```

SETTING UP THE SEARCH FORM

The next part to creating your site is to convert the search form into something useful for information seekers. Begin by actually making it a form and not just a placeholder:

1 Replace

`<p><a name="search">Search form</a></p>`

with the following:

```
<div align="center" class="searchform">
<form method="post" action="/peg">
<a name="search">Search</a>
<input type="text" name="keywords" />
<input type="submit" value="go" />
</form>
</div>
```

To center the search form, you put a div tag around the form tag. Some major browsers don't properly "auto" for margin-right and margin-left. The searchform class helps ensure that the margins are accurate in browsers that support these style sheet features.

2 Prior to the style sheet's --> tag, add the following:

I put a margin of 0 for the actual form tag. For spacing between elements, the value is set to 1em or equal to the default font size in the current browser.

Tip: Although the form tag is an invisible tag, in some browsers, it takes up real estate onscreen because of empty white space. Because the value is set to 0, you don't need to put in the unit: Zero pixels are equal to zero inches.

```
.searchform {
    margin-right: auto;
    margin-left: auto;
    font-weight: bold;
    margin-top: 1em;
    margin-bottom: 1em;
}

form    {
    margin: 0;
}
```

LAYING OUT THE DIRECTORY AND NEWS HEADLINES

The next step to creating your web site is to place the directory and the news headlines in a two-column approach:

1 Apply div tags around the major content chunks in the basic markup:

This takes the content that's earmarked to go on the right side and places a div tag with the class attribute of right_hand. In the next step, you set the style sheet to declare that the right-hand content font size be 80 percent of the default font. The margin on its left side is set to 0 to bump up with the left-hand column.

```
<div class="left hand">

<h3><a name="directory">Web Directory Header</a></h3>

<p>Content of Web Directory</p>

</div>

<div class="right hand">

<h3><a name="headlines">Headlines Header</a></h3>

<p>Content for Hews Headlines</p>

</div>
```

2 Add to the style sheet (after the form):

On the left side, you did a similar process with the div tag in Step 4. However, for left_hand, the style sheet has more activity. You set the font size to be the default size and adjusted the margin to the right to be 20 pixels so that a gutter or space is between the columns. Then you put some padding on the bottom of the section in order to get some white space at the bottom of the page. This helps to avoid the page coming to an end immediately at the end of the content in this section.

```
.left_hand {
        font-size:1em;
        float:left;
        width:67%;
        margin-right:20px;
        padding-bottom:20px;
}

.right_hand {
        font-size:.8em;
        margin-left:0px;
}
```

Note: The real beauty of the style sheet is that the left-hand side *floats* to the left of the right-hand content. The float declaration is similar to aligning an image in HTML to the left or right—the text wraps around the image:

```
<img src="picture.jpg" align="left">
```

Using the float declaration, you ask a content block to wrap around, which causes a visual two-column layout.

3 Place some values for the entire web page in the style sheet:

Here, you set the margin at the top of the page to 0 so the logo image butts against the top of the page. For the left and right side, the margin space is equal to the default size of the font. The primary font choice is set to Verdana, followed by Helvetica, and Arial. If those fonts aren't available to be rendered, the code instructs the computer to pick an available sans-serif font. The page's background color is declared to be white through short hexadecimal notation.

```
body {
    margin:0;
    margin-left: 1em;
    margin-right: 1em;
    font-family: Verdana, Helvetica, Arial, sans-serif;
    background-color: #ffffff;
}
```

MORE MAGIC

If you'd like to add additional interest to your pages, try some of the following recommendations.

Headline News

Want news headlines? They're a popular part of informational sites. Look into Moreover.com. They offer links to articles on subjects from Scandinavia to pop-music reviews, in addition to web-development pieces. When you include links from Moreover.com, the link text is the headline of the article, and the details are available in multiple formats from framesets to XML. The easiest, and least intrusive, method of adding the content to your design is to choose Moreover.com's JavaScript option. This choice gives you the chance to observe the quantity and quality of content Moreover.com distributes while experimenting with layout.

> **Caution:** Although the Moreover.com JavaScript news option is easy to put into action, the main concern if you use it is that people with JavaScript disabled won't be able to see the content. Your awareness of your target audience helps you decide the best route.

Serving Users

If you consider your web site a portal site and are looking for better ways to serve your users, try offering customizable email.

Everyone.net offers a very reasonable pricing structure for services of this kind. What's more, if you'd like a search alternative and community options, take a look at Everyone.net's search and community services.

Challenge Yourself

To add a degree of difficulty to the project in this chapter, build a three-column layout by using CSS. With content wrapped around in `div` tags, create the CSS to have the `div` tags float left—instead of one column floating left with a starting width of 33 percent each. From there, you can play around with widths, background colors, and so on.

Graphic Bullets

Before competent CSS rendering browsers, web developers shied away from nesting unordered item lists. Typically, an unordered list would display a list with inconsistent results in indents. Or the bullet betrayed the aesthetics of the site.

You can create custom graphic bullets for your site, and then, employing the `list-style-image` property, you can call on a graphic bullet of your choice:

```
list-style-image: url(/path/to/imagefile.gif);
```

With CSS, you have the ability to control numerous attributes of the graphic as they relate to the list, including padding and alignment.

Adding Search

Along with such great tools as `moreover.com` and `everyone.net`, you might wish to look at Atomz Search. Atomz offers awesome utilities including freesearch (`www.atomz.com`).

XML FOR THE WIRELESS WEB

"Over the last year in the US, a new

era of mobile freedom has begun thanks

to burgeoning wireless data networks."

—DAVE MOCK

Wireless services are popping up all over the web. Until recently, many webmasters hesitated to serve *Wireless Markup Language* (WML) content to mobile users. They felt that it was too complex, involved a major port of the existing site, or would attract too few users. For some sites, these inhibiting factors are true, but others might be able to provide wireless content with small effort and significant gains.

The technologies used to build wireless web applications are similar to those used in standard web sites. With a few modifications to your server configuration and development techniques, you can serve up applications that are accessible to millions of mobile devices worldwide.

XML for the Wireless Web

By Steve Franklin

PROJECT SNAPSHOT

The problem: Creating content for the wireless web can be confusing at first—even for an experienced web developer. You must understand that a combination of technologies can best empower the individual looking for wireless delivery. Many webmasters are wary of the effort involved in providing WML content from an existing web site. This chapter demonstrates the steps involved in creating a WML application and reviews an approach for serving the same content to WML and HTML without significantly duplicating your effort.

This chapter is for anyone who desires to learn more about creating wireless sites.

TECHNICAL SPECS

The following are the technical specs that you need to use to create wireless web sites:

- **Markup used**—XML

- ***Document type definitions* (DTD) used**—WML 1.3

Here are the additional technologies or skills that you might need:

- Familiarity with HTML

- Basic familiarity with setting up web servers

- Some familiarity with PHP

- Familiarity with a text editor, such as Notepad

How It Works

In this chapter, you will build a sample weather application that reports the weather in regions that the user selects. This application will allow you to show the same data in WML and HTML without duplicating significant amounts of code. By using this approach, you will learn how to deploy information to multiple markup-language formats by using Apache, PHP, and MySQL.

You can build a wireless application in many different ways. One of the most popular means of marking up wireless content is WML, which, similar to XHTML, is an XML DTD. You will use WML for this weather-site project, but a similar approach can work with *Handheld Device Markup Language* (HDML), *Compact Hypertext Markup Language* (CHTML), and other markup languages that are designed for portable devices. More information on WML can be found at www.wapforum.org, including the formal specifications for WML.

To build a successful site, your system will require, at the least, a web server and a wireless device emulator. The web server must be configured to stream pages with the proper *multipurpose Internet mail extensions* (MIME) types. The wireless device emulator will let you browse your newly developed pages, just as your users can see them from their cell phones and *personal digital assistants* (PDAs).

For this chapter, you will also incorporate a database and server-side scripting language. By using a more dynamic approach, it's easier for you to grow your solution and deploy the same data to multiple formats (such as WML, HTML, and so on). Please refer to this book's web site (www.xhtml-resources.com/magic/) for the full working application.

Note: If you're thinking about generating WML content and services for your users, ask yourself the following questions:

- Is my content useful to wireless users?

- Can I attract wireless users to my site's services? Currently, accessing *Wireless Application Protocol* (WAP) can be difficult. However, many service providers are enabling bookmarking of sites through WAP phones and other devices.

- Can I deploy useful content to my users in small pieces to accommodate the currently slow network connections of mobile devices (for example, less than 512 bytes per page)?

If the answers are "Yes," your site might be a good candidate for wireless-ready services.

Set Up Apache and PHP

The first phase of a wireless project is to configure the web server to properly stream back WML, WMLScript, and WML Bitmap files with the proper MIME type. In addition, you will need PHP set up. (If you already did this in Chapter 8, "Creating a Complex Community Site," skip Steps 3 and 4.)

1 Update the MIME configuration file that's found in your `$APACHE_ROOT/conf/mime.types` file or add `AddType` instructions to your `httpd.conf` file:

```
# /opt/apache/conf/mime.types updates to support WML
# delivery with the proper MIME types
image/vnd.wap.wbmp          wbmp  # WML Bitmaps
text/vnd.wap.wmlc           wmlc  # Compiled WML
text/vnd.wap.wmlscriptc     wmlsc # Compiled WMLScript
text/vnd.wap.wml            wml   # WML
text/vnd.wap.wmlscript      wmls  # WMLScript
```

2 Restart Apache, as specified in the Apache manual for your configuration, after these changes are applied.

3 Download and install PHP from `http://www.php.net/`.

4 Integrate PHP with your Apache web server, as described in the PHP installation documentation.

Although the exact procedure depends on your operating system and configuration, it will include updating the default `DirectoryIndex`, adding the PHP application type, and updating the action for handling PHP files through the `httpd.conf` file. Here's an example:

```
# /opt/apache/httpd.conf updates to support PHP
DirectoryIndex index.html index.htm index.shtml index.php
AddType      application/x-httpd-php .php3
AddType      application/x-httpd-php .php4
AddType      application/x-httpd-php .php
AddType      application/x-httpd-php .phtml
Action       application/x-httpd-php "/php"
ScriptAlias /php /usr/bin/php
```

INSTALLING MySQL AND CONFIGURING MySQL SUPPORT

MySQL, a popular relational database, enables you to easily store and retrieve complex information in a reliable fashion. By placing data in MySQL, you can access the same data from different pages without duplicating data. This allows you to eventually report on that same data in WML, HTML, and any other formats you might like to support. To install and configure MySQL, follow these steps:

1   Install MySQL from `http://www.mysql.com/`.

2   Create a new database named "weather" for your wireless application from the command line. To do this, you must launch MySQL from the command prompt that's available within your operating system:

```
% mysql
MySQL> create database weather;
```

3   Configure PHP to support MySQL configuration, as described in the PHP installation documentation.

    If you're compiling PHP from source, you need to include the –with-MySQL=/path/to/MySQL/includes directive. Your php.ini (often installed as /etc/php.ini for Unix or c:\php.ini) must also be updated to point to the MySQL shared library, as shown here:

```
; /etc/php.ini update to point to the MySQL shared library
; The exact details of this section will vary depending on
; your OS and configuration
extension=mysql.so
```

Note: In earlier chapters that covered Apache, the projects assumed that everything was done on a Windows PC. In this chapter, the focus is on open source operating systems. Although you'll have to check with your manuals for individual OS operations, gaining perspective into the various platform differences is a great opportunity to gain multiplatform skills. They'll come in handy as you become more and more advanced in your web building.

SETTING UP THE CLIENT-SIDE DEVELOPMENT ENVIRONMENT

You can set up your client-side development environment by using UP.SDK. UP.SDK can emulate a number of mobile phone environments, which allows you to see how your wireless application looks on a number of commercial phones.

To use UP.SDK:

1 Download and install the UP.SDK at `developer.phone.com`.

> **Note:** Although this project uses the UP.SDK, you can choose from a number of emulators. UP.SDK and Nokia provide the most popular emulator environments, giving you a good spectrum of phone emulations with which to test your code. Nokia's environment can be downloaded from the Application Development area (accessible at `www.nokia.com/wap/`).

2 Run the UP.SDK and navigate existing WAP sites while you are on the Internet.

> **Note:** The UP.SDK only runs on Windows. However, other systems can benefit from web-based emulators that are available from numerous sites, including `www.wapsilon.com` and `www.gelon.net`. These sites can display WML provided that you are running a fairly recent web browser.

Trying the Openwave simulator.

CREATING THE DATA MODEL AND DATABASE TABLES

Although data modeling and database design is beyond the scope of this book, the next phase in any major development project of this nature is to begin building your data models, schemas, and tables. This step can be complicated, but fortunately, some tips, tricks, and resources (in terms of achieving your data goals) are available on this book's web site (www.xhtml-resources.com/magic/).

DESIGNING YOUR APPLICATION

Your application would be easy to design if it consisted solely of a few static WML pages. Instead, you are building a dynamic, data-driven system that requires some planning. The data model is now in place, so it's time to focus on the code that will use this data. Data-driven systems are powerful because they can be changed and extended with minimal effort. It is common to see sites update their "look and feel" in a matter of hours or days. This is because the server-side scripting enabled them to consolidate their *graphical user interface* (GUI) code into a small set of files that are used by all the web pages.

Before you start coding, plan your site's general structure. In your sample application, the entire weather service will consist of one page, which is accessible through http://your.server.com/weather/index.php. Behind the scenes, your weather application will actually be split into a number of files that simplify development, reuse, and future maintenance. Parameters can be passed to this page to specify information on a specific region. Without any parameters, you default to the main page that represents the top-level of your weather application.

Your design must strive for reusable and modular code. You can't anticipate that your code will evolve and grow in the future, but you can defend it against change with a good design. PHP allows you to leverage object-oriented techniques and good programming practices—you should take advantage of these wherever possible.

1 Construct your design so that you separate your rendering code (code that takes data and turns it into a web/wireless page) from the main index.php file.

This ensures that you can easily reuse your code on other pages without having to cut-and-paste it across files.

2 In your application design, separate database access code from the main index.php file and the rendering code in a file called DatabaseObject.inc.

That way, if you change databases, you won't be required to manipulate a large number of files throughout your system.

3 Create specialized code for each output format that you want to support. You can leverage inheritance to allow this.

You might want to generate weather reports in both HTML and WML. You can create a generic WeatherReport program (called a *class* in PHP and in many object-oriented programming languages), which would contain the functionality common to both HTML and WML reports. You then could create two specialized pieces of code: HTMLWeatherReport and WMLWeatherReport. These two files can handle tasks specific to generation of HTML or WML data. These two classes must be written so that they can be used interchangeably by index.php. You can learn more about object-oriented design and development principles at www.cyberdyne-object-sys.com/oofaq2/.

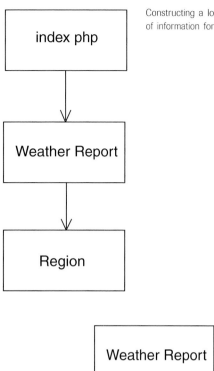

Constructing a logical flow of information for the site.

You can support multiple outputs, including HTML and WML.

4 Factor out common code wherever possible.

The less code you have to rewrite, the better. A number of parts of the application can be factored out:

- Generic database code for managing connections, testing results, building queries, and managing results.
- Rendering code that knows how to build tables, titles, fancy table effects, and so on in a specific markup language.
- "Look and feel" can be pulled into utility classes and style sheets.

It's important that you factor out common code.

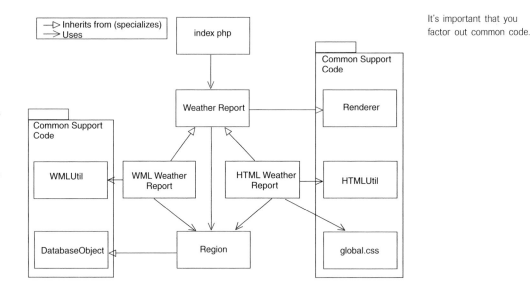

BUILDING YOUR APPLICATION

The top page, index.php performs a simple task: It retrieves a PHP object that knows how to render weather pages. You must write the rendering class WMLWeatherReport to support this. This approach makes the application flexible because you can return different PHP objects, depending on the type of page or look that you want to generate.

You might want to test the parameters passed to your page to see which region the incoming user is requesting. If no variable exists, special behavior is required. The code must then take the incoming variable and use that to extract data from the database. Finally, the code must summarize the data in a WML page and send it back to the browser.

1 Create your index.php file. Upcoming steps will involve creation of the support code that's used by this script.

```
// Code from index.php, representing the top-level of
// our application

// Retrieve a PHP object that we have written to render
// weather pages. The getRenderer(…) function knows how
// to determine what type of browser is asking for the
// page, and can return a suitable renderer that can
```

continues

Your application must detect the incoming browser and determine the appropriate rendering code to use. This code calls on the getRenderer method to obtain the information.

continued

```
// generate HTML, WML, or another format. WML-enabled
// mobile devices have a specific signature that allows
// code to tell them from a Web browser, such as Internet
// Explorer or Netscape.
$renderer = WeatherReport::getRenderer("WeatherReport");

// If the variable $regionId doesn't exist, it wasn't
// passed into the page as a parameter, i.e.
// index.php?regionId=23. We default to region 1 which
// is our "top-level" region with global coverage.
if ( strlen($regionId) <= 0 ) { $regionId = 1; }

$renderer->init($regionId); // Grab data from the database

echo $renderer->getPage();  // Get the WML content and
                            // send it to the browser
```

2 Create the Renderer.inc file to detect the browser type and pick the appropriate code to generate a WML or HTML report:

The getRenderer method determines the browser type by calling on another method, getBrowserType. You do not have to test for the browser type (IE4, NS4, and so on) with this method. Instead, the code must be able to tell the difference between WML- and HTML-compatible browsers. This detection is done by inspecting the HTTP_ACCEPT CGI variable to look for vnd.wap.wml.

The getRenderer function uses a trick to dynamically determine which renderer (WMLWeatherReport or HTMLWeatherReport) should be returned. The getBrowserType method returns WML or HTML. You can use this prefix to dynamically load and return the right class by combining the prefix with the base class name passed into getRenderer as $className. The eval method allows you to execute a command from a string ($str) that you build up.

```
function getRenderer($className) {
  $prefix = Renderer::getBrowserType();

  // Include the appropriate class include
  require($prefix . $className . ".inc");

  // Build up a PHP command string that will be used to
  // create the proper type of object
  $str = "\$renderer=new " . $prefix . $className . ";";

  eval($str);
  return $renderer;
}

function getBrowserType() {
  // Your detection script may have to be more
  // robust and thorough.
  $browserType = getenv("HTTP_ACCEPT");
  $type = "HTML";
  if ( eregi("vnd\.wap\.wml",$browserType) ) {
    $type = "WML";
  }
  return $type;
}
```

3 Create a `Region.inc` file that contains the `Region` class:

Before you start generating the WML pages, you must first query the database to retrieve any required information. Presuming that the user has passed in a valid page and `$regionId` parameter, the `$regionId` can be used to query the database. Rather than put this database code in with the previously identified classes, you created a `Region.inc` file to contain the `Region` class. This class is responsible for retrieving information associated with a region, its weather, and weather alerts.

For the sake of brevity, many details are removed from the code in this step. The samples on this book's web site show the full implementation for the `Region` class. The following list reflects the main highlights of the database code:

- Region subclasses a generic database class (`DatabaseObject`) that you can write to include common DB code, such as the `connect` method.

- To connect, the `DatabaseObject` class should have a method (`setup`) where you can pass in host, username, and database information.

- A "constructor" (a function with the same name as the class) has been written. This constructor automatically runs when an object of type `Region` is created.

- Code in the `queryRegionDetails` method is automatically called when a Region is created because `queryRegionDetails` is called from the constructor.

The implementation of `DatabaseObject.inc` is flexible; you can see some ideas on this book's web site where the full implementation of `DatabaseObject.inc` is contained.

```php
include_once('./support/DatabaseObject.inc');

class Region extends DatabaseObject {
  function Region($newId) {
    $this->setup("localhost","root","weather");
    $this->connect();
    $this->setId($newId);
    $this->queryRegionDetails();
  }

  function queryRegionDetails() {
    // You can test this query directly from MySQL:
    // mysql> SELECT date_format(weatherTime,"%b %d %y")
    // ->    AS weatherTime, temperature
    // ->    FROM RegionWeather WHERE regionId = 8;
    $weatherQuery = "SELECT date_format(weatherTime,";
    $weatherQuery.= "\"%b %d %y\") ";
    $weatherQuery.= "AS weatherTime, temperature ";
    $weatherQuery.= "FROM RegionWeather";
    $weatherQuery.= "WHERE regionId = " . $this->getId();

    $result = mysql_query($weatherQuery);
    if ( mysql_num_rows($result) > 0 ) {
      $row=mysql_fetch_array($result);
      $this->setreportTime($row["weatherTime"]);
      $this->setTemperature($row["temperature"]);
    }
  }

  function setId($newId) { $this->id = $newId;  }
  function getId() { return $this->id; }

  function setreportTime($newreportTime) {
    $this->reportTime = $newreportTime;
  }

  function setTemperature($newTemperature ) {
    $this->temperature = $newTemperature;
  }

  var $id;          // PK for this region.
  var $name;        // Name for this region.
  var $reportTime;  // Time of the weather report
  var $temperature; // Current temperature report
}
```

4 Build your `WMLWeatherReport` class and put it in a file called `WMLWeatherReport.inc`:

The `WMLWeatherReport` class goes in the `WMLWeatherReport.inc` file so that the `getRenderer` method can automatically include it.

Three `include` statements are required to permit calls to `WMLUtil` functions (for formatting and appearance), `Region` objects (for queried data), or methods defined in the `WeatherReport` parent class.

The methods in the `WMLWeatherReport` class reference a number of tags and features of the WML markup language. Because WML is XML-compliant, the strings might look familiar. PHP must build up the WML content by using local variables, and then print the string to the browser. Some common methods (such as `buildBody`, `buildFooter`, and `buildHeader`) come from `WMLUtil.inc`. These functions are common to all WML reports, providing consistent appearance and structure for the header, footer, and contents.

It's likely that you will want to deploy your application to web browsers in addition to mobile users. As a result, you might want to write a `HTMLWeatherReport` class and a corresponding `HTMLUtil.inc` file. These can be similar in appearance to the WML counterparts previously discussed, and you can reuse a significant portion of the database and control code.

```
include('./WeatherReport.inc');    // Parent class
include('./Region.inc');           // Region data object
include('./support/WMLUtil.inc');  // General WML utilities

class WMLWeatherReport extends WeatherReport {
  function report() {
    echo buildHeader(
      getenv(SCRIPT_NAME),$this->getTitle(),
      $this->getKeywords(),$this->getAuthor(),""
    );
    $bodyContents = $this->buildCard($this->region);
    echo buildBody($bodyContents);
    echo buildFooter($this->getAuthor());
  }

  function buildCard($region) {
    $str = "<card>\n   <p>\n";
    $str.= "<u>" . $region->getName();
    $str.= " Weather</u>\n</p>\n";
    $str.= "<p>\n";
    $str.= "   <u>Temp</u>: <b>";
    $str.= $region->getTemperature() . "</b> C<br />\n";
    $str.= $this->getAuthor();
    $str.= "</p>\n</card>\n";
    return $str;
  }
}
```

TESTING THE APPLICATION

During the entire development process, you must regularly view the evolving application to see if your code works as you expected. You can view your application by using the UP.SDK viewer or a browser such as Internet Explorer. Even during the development phase, you should test your code by using a multitude of mobile device emulators to ensure that your code is on the right track and won't require significant rework during the final testing phase. The earlier you can find bugs in your software, the better. To test your application, follow these steps:

1 Launch UP.Simulator from your Windows machine and open one of the phone configurations from the File menu.

By default, the UP.Simulator tries to connect to a test page with a list of WML and HDML sites. You can visit these by using the arrow keys of the mobile phone and the OK button to select a link.

2 Type a server's address in the form `http://site.name/dir/` in the GO field at the top of the UP.Simulator's window. For most of you, the address starts with `http://localhost/...`, as you will be running the server on your development machine.

If the site is not configured to return WML, you receive an error in the emulated phone's display that states, Content-Type Error .... You can check the hidden Phone Information screen to retrieve more information about the error. If you configured your Apache instance correctly, you can point to a sample WML file on your server and display the results.

3 View your new WML application.

If you have an error in your code, the error page streams back as text/html by default. You might want to keep a copy of IE or Netscape running so that you can point at your WML page to get the full error message. For example, if your PHP script won't compile properly, you can sometimes receive the error messages before the MIME type is sent back. Consequently, the PHP error messages will return in a text/html page that UP.Simulator cannot display.

Using the UP.SDK browser.

Viewing the application.

The generated WML code (see Listing 12.1) is shown with the emulated display from the UP.Simulator (see Listing 12.2).

By following the steps in this chapter, you successfully configured a WML-ready web server, set up a database to manage your application's content, and wrote the application that queries the database and returns the information in a format that's suitable for mobile devices. To fit all the steps in this chapter, a number of details were skipped. Although none of these steps are critical to your understanding of the basic concepts and approach of a wireless application, I encourage you to explore the full source code that's included on this chapter's web site (www.xhtml-resources.com/magic/).

LISTING 12.1   A SAMPLE WML PAGE

```
<?xml version="1.0"?>
<!DOCTYPE wml PUBLIC
  "-//WAPFORUM//DTD WML 1.3//EN"
  "http://www.wapforum.org/DTD/wml13.dtd">
<wml>
<head>
  <meta name="keywords" content="Demo"/>
  <meta name="author" content="Us"/>
</head>
<template>
  <do type="accept" label="Loopback">
    <go href="test.wml" />
  </do>
</template><card>
<p>
<u>Demo WML Document</u>
</p>
<p>
  <u>Test</u>:<br />
  <small>Test</small>
</p>
</card>
<card>
<p>This is a second card.</p>
</card>
</wml>
```

LISTING 12.2   A SAMPLE PHP-GENERATED WML PAGE

```
<?xml version="1.0"?>
<!DOCTYPE wml
  PUBLIC "-//WAPFORUM//DTD WML 1.3//EN"
  "http://www.wapforum.org/DTD/wml13.dtd">
<wml>
<head>
  <meta
    name="keywords"
    content="Weather"
  />
```

continues

continued

```
  <meta
    name="author"
    content="WeatherCorp"
  />
</head>
<template>
  <do type="accept" label="Home">
    <go href="/weather/" />
  </do>
  <do type="accept" label="Help">
    <go href="/weather/info.php" />
  </do>
  <do type="accept" label="Misc">
    <go href="/weather/misc.php" />
</do>
</template>
<card>
<p>
  <u>Ottawa Weather</u>
</p>
<p>
  <u>Rainfall Warning</u>
  <a href="#warnings">info</a><br />
  <u>Temp</u>: <b>20.3</b> C<br />
  <u>Barom</u>: <b>101.3</b> kPa<br />
  <u>Wind</u>: <b>15.1</b> km/h<br />
  <u>Vis</u>: <b>25</b> km<br />
```

```
  <u>Precip</u>: <b>80</b> %<br />
  <a href="#obs">Observations</a><br />
  <a href="index.php?regionId=5">
    [Back to Ontario]
  </a><br />
  WeatherCorp
</p>
</card>
<card id="warnings">
<p>
  <u>Warnings for Ottawa</u>
</p>
<p>
  <u>Rainfall Warning:</u>
  Heavy rainfall is expected after dusk
  with increasing winds.<br /><br />
</p>
</card>
<card id="observe">
<p>
  ...
</p>
</card><card>
<p>All contents (c) 2001 WeatherCorp</p>
</card>
</wml>
```

216

More Magic

If you want to continue this application to the point where it is ready for production, you must add a number of steps to make your application work properly:

- Populate the database with a comprehensive set of test data.

- Identify a means of automatically receiving and updating weather information. Weather updates must occur on an hourly basis, so you need to find a suitable (and legitimate) source for this information, as well as a means of entering it into the database. You might be able to find a service provider who can sell you the weather updates in XML (or a similar format).

- Beef up the WML application design to include help pages, cookies, user-configurable options, login, contact information, and peripheral services.

- Test the application under a large spectrum of devices and expose the service to a number of beta users to get real-world feedback.

Also, you might want to modify the application by extending it to support HDML in addition to WML. HDML is still prevalent in North America and Europe. You also might want to consider XHTML Basic and CHTML as other candidate markup languages to support.

INDEX

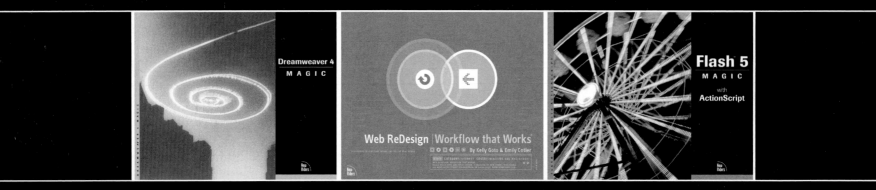

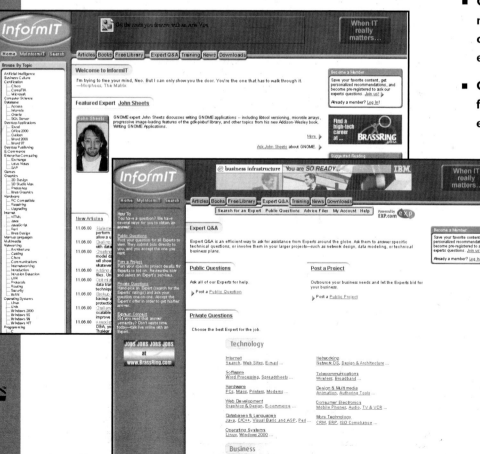

ABOUT THE WEB SITE

You'll want to take advantage of *XML, HTML, XHTML Magic*'s web site offerings. On the site, you'll find the following:

- Information about this book and its goals to clearly address the differences between XML, XHTML, and HTML; defining the contemporary vision of markup from web to wireless; using a variety of markup combined with CSS to address contemporary design issues; and integrating technologies, including JavaScript and PHP, with markup to demonstrate real-world problems and easy solutions.

- Biographies about (and insights from) this book's authors.

- All sample code and graphic files necessary to work through this book's projects.

- Book updates and corrections.

- A feedback option so you can tell the authors and publisher what you think of this book.

- A list of recommended resources for evolving web designers.

Drop by www.xhtml-resources.com/magic/ today!